CAREERS
FOR
PUZZLE SOLVERS
& Other Methodical Thinkers

VGM Careers for You Series

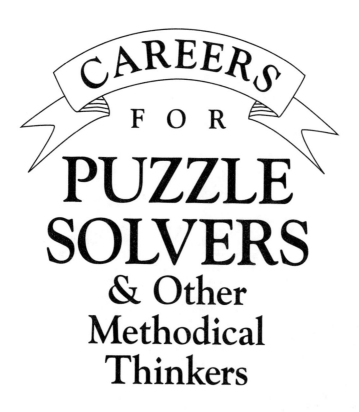

CAREERS FOR
PUZZLE SOLVERS
& Other Methodical Thinkers

Jan Goldberg

VGM Career Books

Chicago New York San Francisco Lisbon London Madrid Mexico City
Milan New Delhi San Juan Seoul Singapore Sydney Toronto

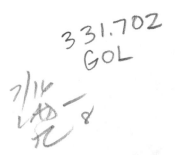

VGM Career Books

A Division of The McGraw·Hill Companies

ISBN 0-658-00180-9 (hardcover)
       0-658-00181-7 (paperback)

This book was set in Goudy Old Style by ImPrint Services
Printed and bound by Lake Book Manufacturing

This book is dedicated to my
very special husband, Larry,
and my precious daughters,
Sherri and Debbie. Thank
you for bringing so much joy
into my life.

Contents

Acknowledgments

The author gratefully acknowledges:

- The numerous professionals who graciously agreed to be profiled in this book

- My dear husband, Larry, for his inspiration and vision

- My daughters, Sherri and Deborah, for their encouragement and love

- Family and close friends—Adrienne, Marty, Mindi, Cary, Michele, Paul, Michele, Alison, Steve, Marci, Steve, Brian, Steven, Jesse, Andy, Colin, Bertha, and Aunt Helen—for their faith and support

- Diana Catlin, for her insights and input

- Editors Denise Betts and Betsy Lane, for making all projects rewarding and enjoyable

CHAPTER ONE

Introduction

When I'm working on a problem, I never think about beauty. I think only how to solve the problem. But when I have finished, if the solution is not beautiful, I know it is wrong.   R. BUCKMINSTER FULLER

A mother is watching from across the room as her four-year-old son tries desperately to retrieve the coins that he just deposited into his new piggy bank. He stares at the bank for a moment, then shakes it vigorously. He frowns, then turns it upside down and shakes it again. His scowl deepens as he tugs on the pig's ears, tries to twist its nose, even tries fitting his fingers into the coin slot on top. After several minutes of trial and error, he finally notices the rubber stopper on the bottom. With one firm tug, the stopper comes out, and the coins spill onto the floor. "Mommy, I did it!" he squeals with delight, beaming from ear to ear.

His mother smiles proudly, wondering what great future awaits her son. At his young age, he's already practicing the puzzle-solving skills and methodical thinking that will one day come in handy as he decides which career path to follow.

There are many exciting careers that require the uncovering of clues and other evidence. Such clue gathering is then followed by applying one's skills and experience to put all the evidence together in order to come to a logical conclusion, solve a problem or puzzle, or fix something that is broken. You could say, then, that this book is all about detectives. Private investigators are discussed, of course, but you'll also find profiles of several other careers that employ similar clue-gathering and interpretation methods.

Do you think you'd be good at solving puzzles for a living? Find out if you have what it takes by answering true or false to the following statements.

1. When presented with a problem, I can usually think of more than one way it might be solved.

2. I would welcome the challenge of trying to solve a puzzle that no one has been able to solve before.

3. I am patient long after most people would have given up.

4. The process of trial and error doesn't frustrate me; it challenges me to work harder!

5. Sometimes I take things apart just to see if I can put them back together again.

6. If I were having a hard time solving a puzzle, I would keep at it until I figured it out.

7. I am always looking for new challenges.

8. I am willing to pursue a career that requires that I continually stay abreast of the latest trends and/or advancements in my field.

9. I never get bored when working on the same project for a long time.

10. I don't give up easily.

11. I can usually turn on a dime and change my way of thinking quickly if my first approach to solving a problem doesn't work out.

12. I'm known for always thinking logically.

13. I'm fascinated by the way all the pieces of a puzzle fit together so neatly.

If most of these statements were true for you, you're probably a born puzzle solver! Even if just a handful of them are true, it sounds as if you'll benefit from the information presented in this book. You'll learn all about what it takes to become an archaeologist, architect, automobile mechanic, private investigator, engineer, computer scientist, doctor, inventor, investigative reporter, research scientist, or interior designer. Though this list of careers is seemingly very diverse, they all have one important element in common: they all rely heavily on puzzle solving and methodical thinking skills.

So let's get started in solving our first puzzle: which career path *you* might choose to follow!

Nothing in this world can take the place of persistence. Talent will not; nothing is more common than unsuccessful people with talent. Genius will not; unrewarded genius is almost a proverb. Education will not; the world is full of educated derelicts. Persistence and determination alone are omnipotent. The slogan 'press on' has solved and always will solve the problems of the human race. CALVIN COOLIDGE

For every problem, there is a solution that is simple, neat, and wrong. HENRY LOUIS MENCKEN

The problems that exist in the world today cannot be solved by the level of thinking that created them. ALBERT EINSTEIN

CHAPTER TWO

Careers in Interior Design

Always design a thing by considering it in its next larger context—a chair in a room, a room in a house, a house in an environment, an environment in a city plan. ELIEL SAARINEN

Help Wanted: Interior Designer

We are seeking an interior designer to work full-time for our firm in Arizona. Candidates will be expected to develop and execute a broad spectrum of office-planning projects, maintain control of project costs, and work with senior office-planning staff to assure compliance to all company and governmental regulations.

Requirements include a minimum of three years' experience in office planning, furniture specification, and building-finishes selection. Candidates must also possess the ability to plan and execute office construction and renovation projects. Superior interpersonal skills, the ability to work independently, knowledge of various office furniture brands (such as Herman Miller, Knoll, and Steel Case), and pharmaceutical experience are desired. The job offers a generous benefit package.

Zeroing In on What an Interior Designer Does

If you have a flair for color, shape, balance, pattern, and room furnishings, then interior design may be a perfect fit for your future!

Interior designers design living and working spaces. Glamorous portrayals of the profession show interior designers happily flitting about mansions, absorbing the "flow" of the place and discussing curtains. But interior designers are actually responsible for the entire inside of a building—the design, decoration, and functionality of it, whether it's residential, commercial, or industrial. They are concerned with keeping form, color, scale, and arrangement in balance, and they must be familiar with current trends as well as historical periods that have influenced furniture styles and room design. They must be certain that the design works for its purpose; if a building's pattern of entrances and exits made no sense to the occupants, it would be a failure. Interior designers must also ensure that the building's inside relates to its outside; a building constructed for use as an industrial warehouse, for instance, would not have an interior design like that of a luxury home.

This profession falls somewhere between a decorator and an architect, for interior designers not only have to know which paint colors and fabrics will look best, but also which walls can be torn down without causing structural damage or where the public rest rooms should be located in an office building. In fact, in some European countries where interior design is a more established profession, it is called interior architecture.

The puzzle that interior designers solve every day is trying to fit their experience, creativity, and good judgment together with the desires and requirements of their clients, while also making everything look attractive, function properly, and stay within budget. And, it all must be in accordance with federal, state, and local laws, taking into account such things as building codes, flammability and toxicity standards, and accessibility. In fact, interior design is the only design field subject to governmental regulations; like doctors and architects, in some states interior designers are required to be licensed in order to practice the profession.

Because they often begin their work before a building is completed, interior designers have to know how to think like architects, using blueprints to guide them as they prepare sketches and models of their designs. Once those designs are approved by their clients, it's time for meetings (with plumbers, electricians, and other contractors) and shopping (for furniture, wall coverings, floor coverings, and window treatments)—all while making sure every aspect of the project is taken care of, clients are satisfied, directions are being followed, and they are not spending more money than that which has been authorized.

Those who have been in the field a long time and those who are new to it share a common challenge: dealing with difficult clients who might not understand why their vision of how they want their building's interior to look cannot be made a reality due to structural, financial, or other concerns. This is where an interior designer's people skills come into play. Some clients also demand that the interior designers they hire are available whenever they need them, which often results in working long or irregular hours and on weekends. However, experienced and successful interior designers may enjoy many perks, like contact with high-profile and/or wealthy clients, substantial salaries, and frequent travel to meet with clients or to shop for new materials at wholesale markets.

On the Job

People are busier these days than ever before, and many just don't have the time to design and decorate their homes and work spaces. However, because the hiring of an interior designer is still considered by some to be a luxury expense, jobs are more plentiful during prosperous times.

Fledgling designers usually receive on-the-job training for two or three years. Once designers are licensed, there are numerous paths to follow within the two major categories—residential and commercial. Within each are specialized fields and subspecialties. An interior designer might choose to become a project manager, draftsperson, or specifier of products. One might decide to concentrate on restaurants or residential baths or to specialize even further and design only airplane interiors. A professional might choose to become an expert in another subspecialty, such as lighting, fabrics, or historical restorations.

According to the Bureau of Labor Statistics, "designers of all types are nearly four times as likely to be self-employed as are other specialty professionals," so many interior designers do eventually move on to owning and operating their own design studios. For those who would rather work for someone else, though, there are plenty of opportunities.

Interior designers employed at large design firms often work toward becoming chief designers or department heads. Large architecture firms often have separate interior design departments, home furnishings stores employ interior designers to help customers make decisions, and universities or art schools hire interior design professionals to teach. Those who choose to leave the interior design field often choose another design-related profession and become interior decorators or graphic artists. Some return to school in order to become architects.

Wherever there are people, there is interior design work to be found. However, jobs will be more plentiful near large metropolitan areas that have more clients and larger budgets. The most elite firms in the country are located in New York City, Chicago, Los Angeles, and Atlanta.

Qualifications and Training

A healthy mix of personality traits, natural talents, and acquired skills are required for individuals who seek to become successful interior designers.

At the top of the list, interior designers must be good listeners, analytical thinkers, and problem solvers. In fact, they must be visionaries—for the frequent times when they are faced with having to interpret the sometimes vague or unrealistic expectations of their clients. Besides having a natural eye for color, texture, fashion, spatial relations, and the intuition to know what a client wants, candidates must also have specialized knowledge of structural engineering and basic architectural principles. This is not a profession for anyone who is disorganized. Interior designers must be detail-oriented individuals and effective multitaskers, as well as creative, outgoing, and disciplined personalities.

Since licensing is not mandatory in all states, membership in a professional association is the most recognized mark of achievement in the profession. This is because such memberships usually require the completion of three or four years of postsecondary education in design, at least two years of practical experience, and completion of the National Council for Interior Design (NCID) qualification exam. Therefore, candidates should take the exam even if the state they work in doesn't require it because it will assure them a high level of credibility and professionalism.

The postsecondary education required is usually a bachelor of arts or bachelor of fine arts degree. Though a liberal arts education—with classes in merchandising, business administration, marketing, and psychology—is a good background, B.F.A. programs are more geared to the profession, as they include art, art history, computer-aided design, textiles, mechanical and architectural drawing, sculpture, and basic engineering. Formal training is also available at two- and three-year professional schools that award certificates or associates degrees in interior design. More than one hundred colleges and universities in the United States offer programs that have been accredited by the Foundation for Interior Design Education Research (FIDER).

Beginning interior designers usually receive on-the-job training for two or three years—working as an assistant or intern. Though salaries at this stage are often minimal or nonexistent, candidates should understand that they are gaining valuable experience and developing comprehensive portfolios that will help them secure good positions later. (A good portfolio will include sketches and preliminary designs as well as photos of completed projects.)

Throughout their careers, interior designers can keep up on the latest trends by staying active in their professional associations and subscribing to design and architectural magazines.

Salaries

Salaries for interior designers vary widely depending on the type of responsibilities required, whether they are self-employed or salaried, years of experience, reputation, demand, and regional differences.

Initially, designers can expect to earn about $20,000 to $30,000 per year. Midlevel designers with three or more years' experience can anticipate making a bit more, perhaps $35,000 to $40,000. Designers with good project-management skills can command substantially higher salaries, $50,000 to $55,000 in the role of managers. Top interior designers can earn $75,000 to $100,000 per year or more.

Meet and Greet

Nina L. Nielsen

"Prior to founding NS Designs with Sandra Harding, I was senior design associate at Alternative Design, where I headed the environments division," says Nielsen. "I was recruited to develop an interior design residential department, where I managed a staff of interior designers, graphic designers, and production personnel on the residential designs for some of the most high-profile entertainers in the country. Prior to joining Alternative Design, I was the manager of interiors for the premier retailer Tiffany & Company, where I was responsible for creating and maintaining a new division within the store planning department. My responsibilities included the interior design and renovation of new locations, along with existing locations worldwide, overseeing jobs budgeting more than $2 million per location.

"Prior to Tiffany & Company, I was the project manager of wholesale and international in-store planning for the Nine West Group, as well as the interiors project manager at Naomi Leff & Associates, where I designed and project managed high-end residential projects for Oscar award–winning actors and producers. I have a bachelor's degree in interior design from the Fashion Institute of Technology.

"At NS Designs, we specialize in residential and commercial design, although our current projects are mostly residential. We are designing an apartment in New York City (with an amazing view of the Hudson River) for a writer and artist, as well as an apartment on the Upper East Side of Manhattan, and a loft in Brooklyn.

"My mother is a fashion designer, so art is what I grew up with. In keeping with this, I attended a specialized music and art high school and thought I was going to be an art historian or art gallery owner. When I started looking into colleges, I stumbled across New York School of Interior Design and instinctively felt that this was the ideal place for me. At that moment, I knew that interior design was what I wanted to do. It combined all of the arts together—color, space, and composition on the biggest canvas you can imagine.

"In this field, there are so many surprises, every day is a challenge, especially when you own your own company. In fact, my largest challenge was to start my own company. As Gordon Parks is quoted as saying, 'The guy who takes a chance, who walks the line between the known and unknown, who is unafraid of failure, will succeed.'

"Puzzle solving is what interior design is all about. We have created the maze, and we have to guide people through the space allotted. In design, all the variables have to add up. There must be a definite plan with a beginning and an end (or an entrance and an exit). Your approach must be sequential—you must do certain things before you start the next, or you have to backtrack.

"For me, the best part of interior design is when you walk a client through their new space at the end of the project. If it is a residential project, we like to first set the mood—doing things such as lighting scented candles and dimming the lights. We have even gone as far as to have the clients' chef prepare their favorite meal so that when they walk into the house, the aroma of food lingers throughout. Just seeing when the client finally *gets it* because they finally see it, that's the best part of what we do.

"The best advice I've ever gotten is to 'feel the fear and do it anyway,' and this is now the screen saver on my computer. I would also recommend that those interested in the interior design field should attempt to work for different types of companies. There are so many facets to this field, you'll learn different things in varying situations. For instance, try to work for a residential firm and/or a contract firm, or try health care. Once you gain experience in different types of design, you will find your niche."

Sandra Harding

Sandra Harding is an interior designer and the coprincipal of NS Designs in New York City.

"When I was twelve years old, I took a drafting and methods and materials of construction class and then followed up with similar classes in high school," says Harding. "In my junior year, I tossed around the idea of studying architecture, but then I realized that I also wanted to do something more creative, so I chose interior design.

"I attended the Fashion Institute of Technology and obtained my bachelor of fine arts degree. After Nina and I worked on our first project together (an apartment on Central Park West), we both realized that we should first work for other people to gain the knowledge that's needed to work in the 'real world.' So, I landed a position as assistant interior designer for Six Flags Theme Parks. I designed complete interior and visual packages, as well as managed installations for branded retail shops and restaurants for the company's six theme parks. I then worked as a freelance visual merchandiser for both Tiffany & Company and Bloomingdale's, and then as project manager for another firm, designing and managing high-end residential interior design projects in affluent Long Island communities.

"Just prior to starting NS Designs full-time, I spent two years as senior designer and director of operations for a design/build and management firm, where I was responsible for the direction and creative processes of space planning and design of residential and commercial health clubs and spas for New York's most prominent real estate developers. I supervised construction and consulted with the owners, architects, and contractors on the specifications and technical details involved in building clubs. As part of my operational responsibilities, I proposed new concepts and marketing tools for club renovations and maintaining yearly capital expenditures.

"In 1999, Nina and I set up all of the necessary paperwork to start our company, NS Designs. Although we were still working for others at the time, we were always out there, trying to find clients and making our names known to others. Happily, on January 1, 2000, we began to devote full-time hours to our company. Right now, we are working on three residential interior design projects and also as stylists for the 'Living & Style' section of a popular monthly publication.

"Surprises in this profession are the everyday glitches that we need to catch before the client is aware that there may be a momentary problem. The challenge is helping the client visualize the final product, although with a small investment, computer aides help.

"Problem solving and methodical thinking are words that describe this profession perfectly. We design space and we must create layouts for all that is needed for the project. We must specify and come up with all viable solutions to create a complete interior environment to ensure that our ideas can become a reality.

"The best part of the job is the creative aspect and the fact that every project can be approached as its own entity. Another treat is the fact that the creative process is always new—with fresh ideas for every project. This leaves no time for boredom.

"The best advice I ever received is to do what I truly enjoy and to go after my dreams and ambitions. That's exactly what I've done."

Deborah Burnett

Deborah Burnett is the president of Design Service, Inc., in Springfield, Tennessee.

"I've learned to survive as a creative being and then thrive as a female businessperson by first developing my creative, imaginative, and human side, and then by adding a strong input of right-side skills," says Burnett. "Consequently, my education and career path have been diverse and unique. As a college-bound academic student in high school, I also elected to study at the local vo-tech facility in the field of graphic design and drafting. I then attended Edinboro University, where I studied art history and architecture.

"Not realizing my passion for human involvement, I then studied and graduated from LaSalle University in Philadelphia with a degree in psychiatric social work, where I fulfilled my inner desire to explore the human experience. As for working in that field? I lasted a whole day in the Philadelphia welfare department! As I'd already had enough of low-pay human experiences, my practical side kicked in. So, I became the youngest IBM sales representative in the country. It seems that my creative reasoning, coupled with my business acumen and abstract thinking skills, garnered me a position with the largest and most prestigious company in the world.

"With IBM, aside from fine-tuning my rational thinking processes, I also learned to develop several valuable life skills lessons in the marketing and self-promotion department. These are the skills that later would prove to be the most beneficial when I was struggling with a fledgling career in interior design and construction. I grew up around construction, was innately creative, learned to develop an insight into the needs and desires of people seeking to improve their lives, and was able to market myself and make money. So, enter the field of interior design; it was a natural career choice for me. And the funny thing is that the decision was made without my even realizing what was happening. It seemed that everything I had done up to that point was in direct preparation for the role I now have. I see this to be impacting people's lives as it relates to their homes and offices and, ultimately, how they feel about themselves.

"As a registered interior designer and licensed building contractor, my work has helped to further promote my deep belief that creating a comfortable home and office is not difficult once you know the basics. My job the past twenty years has been not only to create and implement a comfortable environment for my clients, but to also teach. I have found that the simple act of teaching the basics of creativity and design so that others may learn to appreciate the beauty and satisfaction of a truly comfortable surrounding is the life mission I have developed for myself.

"I've always been a creative thinker and have enjoyed the creative process. As a child of the sixties, I literally grew up with the first girls-only self-esteem play icon, Barbie. Early on, I realized she needed a home, so even as a young child, I began to create elaborate and functional multilevel homes for my dolls. Using numerous folding tables and cardboard boxes to re-create floor space, I filled her house with shoe-box sofas, soap-filled glass-jar washing machines, and fabric-scrap area rugs. For me, the creation of these 'homes' was more fun than the actual doll play. I was hooked—designing, creating, and facilitating dreams into reality was, and still is, my identity and life's work.

"I believe that every human is a unique mystery and that his or her dreams and expectations of life's comforts are no exception. Trying to unravel a person's dreams, plans, and scattered thoughts for a comfortable and fashionable home and office is like trying to contain, analyze, and then create a cloud.

"The puzzle of weaving the client's ever-changing mind's-eye dream into the finished project containing bricks, fabric, and furnishings is a tough job—like trying to rope a cloud and put a box around it, getting it done for less than what you know it should cost.

"Developing a functional left-side skill level, along with basic business understanding, is the key ingredient to any career choice, most importantly for those seeking employment in the creative design arena. Even though it's hard for us creative right-side types to fathom, the actual day-to-day profession of interior design is only about 15 percent creative, while a full 85 percent of the time is spent in utilizing the learned skills of problem solving, number crunching, and organizational pursuits. In other words, trying to create and then organize, budget, and facilitate 'nothing' into a beautiful 'something' is hard work, requiring skills that do not always come naturally to the creative spirit. But I see my mission as opening the eyes of humankind to the beauty of the world via the route of personal comfort."

For Additional Information

National Council for Interior Design Qualification
1200 Eighteenth Street NW, Suite 1001
Washington, DC 20036
www.ncidq.org

American Society of Interior Designers
608 Massachusetts Avenue NE
Washington, DC 20002
www.asid.org

Foundation for Interior Design Education Research
60 Monroe Center NW, Suite 300
Grand Rapids, MI 49503
www.fider.org

CHAPTER THREE

Careers in Archaeology

Digging up the past.   LEONARD WOOLEY, ON HIS PASSION

> ## Help Wanted: Staff Archaeologist
> We are seeking a staff archaeologist for full-time work with our company in Las Vegas, Nevada. Responsibilities include conducting literature reviews and site record searches; preparing reports, including descriptive text and tabulating and analyzing field data; using and interpreting topographic maps; and acting as assistant crew chief and crew member for field surveys, testing, and data recovery. Advanced writing and communication skills are essential. Candidate must be conversant with the secretary of the interior's criteria for evaluation of significance, must be willing to travel (possibly extensively), and to work in difficult field settings. Job benefits include medical and dental insurance, sick leave, vacation pay, and a 401(k).

Zeroing In on What an Archaeologist Does

If you think that an archaeologist digs stuff up, dusts it off, stares at it for a while, then puts it under glass in a museum, you may be surprised to learn how multifaceted this field actually is!

Archaeology is a branch of anthropology, which is the scientific study of the development of human beings within societies.

19

Archaeology, however, concentrates only on the *material remains* of those societies—the human (not dinosaur) bones, primitive tools, pottery fragments, and building ruins, for instance, that were left behind. By examining these material things, archaeologists gain insight into the human ways of the past and how they relate to the human ways of the present.

A strong curiosity about the secrets of the past is a must for those wishing to pursue a career in archaeology. Archaeologists are like private investigators, searching for clues and looking for answers, whether they're working high on a mountainside in Chile, in an underground cave in Kansas, or deep under the Atlantic. Depending on the project, they may be studying artifacts from prehistoric times or from the 1880s.

Archaeology is not always as exciting as an *Indiana Jones* movie; it is actually one of the most demanding branches of the social sciences. Archaeologists might find themselves digging strenuously for days (resulting in sore muscles, cuts, and bruises) or spending months systematically cataloging thousands of nearly identical artifacts (resulting in possible boredom). Because many of the best excavation sites are located in temperate zones, archaeologists often spend full days working in the hot sun. And, if they're at a remote site far from home, they must also adapt to living in another country, perhaps one without all the amenities they're accustomed to having. Through their work, however, archaeologists have a chance to make exciting, headline-news discoveries about ancient peoples (like the worldwide sensation that Howard Carter caused when he discovered King Tut's tomb in 1922). They then get to share their work with the world by showcasing their findings in special museum exhibits.

Qualifications and Training

Successful archaeologists must possess a natural curiosity about the past and how it relates to the present. They must also be adventurous, hard working, adaptable, and unafraid of getting their hands dirty. Additionally, an ability to discern slight differences in pattern and color is important, along with expertise in using computers.

As is the case with most scientific fields, a bachelor's degree is insufficient. A complete program of graduate study is usually necessary. Most professional archaeologists have a master's degree, and a sizeable number have doctorates.

A bachelor's degree is often earned in anthropology, since only a small number of schools have a separate archaeology department (though that number is growing all the time). Besides the degree's required courses, students also find that nearly any other course will prove to be helpful in some way, from physics and biology to sociology and art history. Because producing research papers and field reports is a big part of the job, writing, word processing, and desktop publishing also come in handy. Additionally, scuba-diving skills are necessary for those who wish to pursue a career in underwater archaeology.

Fortunately, though, because of archaeology's broad scope, an undergraduate degree in nearly any discipline will be useful. Archaeologists often earn bachelor's degrees in geology, history, zoology, geography, botany, linguistics, chemistry, and many other fields.

More than five hundred United States colleges and universities offer master's degrees in anthropology and/or its branches, and more than a hundred of these have programs that lead to a doctorate. Aside from regular course work and fieldwork, knowledge of at least one language other than the candidate's native language will probably be required. The choice of language will depend on future aspirations; someone who hopes to one day be the curator of a museum in Berlin might favor German, while Spanish would likely be the language of choice for someone who wants to excavate ancient ruins in South America.

When choosing a school, candidates should keep in mind the differences between a small school and a large university and choose the one that better meets their needs. A smaller school will have a more relaxed atmosphere and perhaps less competition, while a larger school will offer more opportunities for field-work but also more demands and more competition.

What's most important in choosing a program, however, is finding one that emphasizes the candidate's particular area(s) of interest within the field. Those wishing to specialize in a certain geographic area or time period of history will want to find a school with adequate resources to support that interest.

A good deal of study will also happen in the field, where valuable experience is gained in the general principles of field research, including how to dig properly, accurately record data, preserve artifacts, and prepare site maps. Candidates will also discover how many seemingly unrelated skills will come in handy—such as first aid, photography, public relations, and even auto mechanics. Those new to the field can expect to be assigned the menial tasks, but it's important to obtain as much field experience as possible.

Continued training throughout an archaeologist's career is important, as new methods and tools for gathering and examining artifacts and other information are continually being developed. Each state has at least one archaeological society, and membership can provide archaeologists with a way to interact with peers, visit historical sites, and attend lectures, seminars, and workshops.

On the Job

Although early archaeologists were seen mainly as hobbyists, self-funded or supported by wealthy benefactors, the field has grown and changed considerably during the last century. It has become accepted as a legitimate profession, particularly due to the fact that it is recognized as essential to the planning process for new construction.

The different areas that an archaeologist can specialize in are practically unlimited, with the two main branches being *terrestrial* and *underwater*. The latter is relatively new, having only been fully developed during the twentieth century. *Historical archaeology* focuses on the period of recorded history after humans learned to write, while *prehistoric archaeology* studies humanity's past before written communication was developed. Within each of these areas, archaeologists can also specialize in certain geographic areas, such as the Mediterranean or Central America, or in certain time periods, such as Paleozoic or Medieval. In addition, archaeologists can specialize in different methods, such as excavation, classification, or preservation.

According to a recent study, about 38 percent of working archaeologists are employed at colleges and universities, 24 percent in private firms, 18 percent in government agencies, and 10 percent in museums.

Colleges and universities employ archaeologists who teach courses in their own fields and often in anthropology and history as well. They also devote time to fieldwork and other research and are expected to publish articles based on their research in academic journals. When they're not on campus, they can probably be found far away from home working on a dig.

Archaeologists often work for private consulting firms or major corporations whose work could possibly cause rare historical artifacts to be displaced or even destroyed. These archaeologists are part of the planning process for new construction, writing environmental impact statements and ensuring that records and collections are cared for properly.

Federal and state government agencies, such as the Bureau of Land Management and the National Park Service, require archaeologists to assist them in managing the archaeological resources that fall under their jurisdictions or those that might be affected by their programs.

Archaeologists working as museum curators undertake the task of managing and caring for the institution's entire collection of artifacts. This includes, but is not limited to, deciding how best to restore, care for, display, store, research, and keep track of the museum's collection. Historic buildings, monuments, and other preserved sites often have archaeologists on staff as well.

Those who choose to leave the somewhat competitive field of archaeology often go on to a related field where their archaeological knowledge can be put to good use, such as surveying, linguistics, or history. Those who major in archaeology without wanting to pursue a career in the field are attractive to potential employers in a wide variety of fields; archaeology effectively combines the arts and the sciences, thereby producing graduates who are able to write and communicate well while also understanding technology.

Salaries

According to the Bureau of Labor Statistics, archaeologists, as part of the larger occupation of social scientists, earn an average of approximately $33,000 per year.

Starting salaries for college and university teaching positions usually range from $25,000 to $40,000. With considerable experience and a Ph.D., an archaeologist could earn $60,000 to $80,000.

Meet and Greet

Sharon F. Urban

Sharon F. Urban is a public archaeologist for the Arizona State Museum in Tucson, where she is responsible for maintaining the archaeological state files. She has three degrees: an A.A., a B.A., and an M.A. Her field experience includes working as a highway salvage archaeologist for six years, and her specialties are the analysis of shell artifacts from Southwestern sites and the recording, study, and analysis of Southwestern rock art. Sharon knew she wanted to be an archaeologist ever since elementary school, when she studied the La Brea Tar Pits.

"My biggest surprise was discovering a painted set of ceramic vessels, and my largest challenge has been learning the computer," Urban says. "What archaeologists dig up are only the hard parts of a culture. We need to put them together to create that past culture. What we find are bits and pieces of a puzzle, which have to be reconstructed into a whole so as to determine what they are, what they are made out of, how they were made, and how everything functioned.

"The best part of the job is reconstructing a culture from bits and pieces. I also particularly enjoy the fieldwork and the act of discovery. Working outside and teaching others what you have learned are also rewarding.

"As far as advice goes, I would say that if you are interested in becoming an archaeologist, then do so! Don't let anyone talk you out of it. At least go to a field school and give it a try. If you do not like it, then little time was wasted in finding that out. It's true that you may not get rich in archaeology. Nevertheless, I don't know any archaeologist who does not like his or her job."

Penny Dufoe Minturn

Penny Minturn is a bioarchaeologist for Bioarch in Payson, Arizona. After studying forestry and recreational therapy at the University of Missouri for three years, she went on to earn a B.A. in anthropology and an M.A. in bioarchaeology, both from Arizona State University. She is currently studying for her Ph.D. in physical anthropology.

"I have nineteen years of experience in archaeology, starting as a laborer and working my way up—crew member, assistant crew chief, crew chief, assistant field director, assistant project director," Minturn explains. "Currently, I own my own company, called Bioarch. We specialize in the identification, recovery, analysis, and reporting of burial features. I would estimate that 70 percent of my training came in doing fieldwork, and the other 30 percent from school. However, I would not be able to do the work I do without having had both types of training.

"I am currently at work on several projects in Arizona. I sub-contract with archaeology companies who are working on sites along highway corridors; we are in charge of mitigating all human remains at these sites. Although excavating a burial is similar in many ways to digging up other kinds of features, there are also many things about them that merit special attention. I am in charge of making sure they get that special attention.

"I have always loved history and stories about real people. I never really considered a career in archaeology, though, until I moved to Arizona. Arizona State University's anthropology department was excavating near where I lived, and they were looking for local people to help. I thought it sounded like fun, so I went out to the site and talked to the archaeologists, who showed me around. In no time, I was completely captivated, quit my part-time job, started working at the site the following day, and have done nothing but archaeology since. There is absolutely nothing like the feeling of 'touching the past.'

"The biggest surprise has been how much I enjoy public speaking now. At one time, I was very shy, but I love archaeology so much that standing in front of people and talking about what I do is a real joy. It has helped me come out of my shell. The biggest challenge has been as a woman trying to be a professional and have a family, too. It has been a challenge but worth every minute of it.

"Puzzle solving and methodical thinking are absolutely crucial to archaeology. Basically, what you are doing is finding pieces of the past (either pieces of houses, pottery, projectile points, burial customs, or a million other possibilities), and you have to look at what you have and put it back together in a way that makes sense. You have to take the physical information you have, apply what you know from other studies and other disciplines, and try to come up with a picture that's logical.

"Deciding what I like best is the hardest part—there are so many things that are great. Probably for me, the best part is working with so many great people who share my enthusiasm for what we do. Archaeology can be physically hard, intellectually demanding, and occasionally quite frustrating. People don't become archaeologists because it's easy or because they expect to make lots of money. So you find that you share a mind-set, a certain outlook on life, a definite *joie de vivre* with the people you work with. Besides all the other great things about archaeology, it's just plain *fun*! In addition, archaeology has allowed me to work in so many beautiful places, like the San Juan Mountains of Colorado, the Grand Canyon, Santa Ana and Hermosillo in Mexico, and Abydos in Egypt. The opportunities are amazing!

"My advice is to go to school, but be sure to get hands-on experience, too. Learning from others is a great idea, but never forget to think for yourself."

For Additional Information

Archaeological Institute of America
656 Beacon Street, Fourth Floor
Boston, MA 02215
www.archaeological.org

Society for American Archaeology
900 East Second Street NE, Number Twelve
Washington, DC 20002
www.saa.org

Center for American Archeology
P.O. Box 22
Kampsville, IL 62053
www.caa-archeology.org

Center for the Study of Architecture/Archaeology
P.O. Box 60
Bryn Mawr, PA 19010
www.csanet.org

CHAPTER FOUR

Careers in Engineering

Something is wrong if workers do not look around each day, find things that are tedious or boring, and then rewrite the procedures. Even last month's manual should be out of date. TOYOTA: TAICHI OHNO

Help Wanted: Staff Engineer

Our company develops and markets innovative products for surgeons, such as sutures and ligatures. In this role, you will assess new technologies and product opportunities. This will involve focusing on intellectual property, feasibility of approach, product safety, and technical alternatives. You'll oversee collaborations with external technology sources, lead the incorporation of new technologies, develop prototypes, and provide technical training for your work group.

To qualify, you must have a Ph.D. in engineering or physics and one to two years of product design and development experience, preferably with medical devices. Thorough knowledge of the product development process is a must. The successful candidate will also have strong presentation, communication, and interpersonal skills.

As a valued team member, you'll receive a competitive salary and great benefits, including medical/dental, a 401(k), a pension plan, and a comprehensive wellness program. Please apply directly on-line at our website.

Zeroing In on a Career in Engineering

Engineers apply the theories and principles of science and mathematics to the economical solution of practical technical problems. Usually their work is the link between a scientific discovery and its commercial application. Engineers design machinery, products, systems, and processes for efficient and economical performance.

Engineers consider many factors in developing a new product. For example, in developing an industrial robot, they determine precisely what function it needs to perform; design and test the necessary components; fit them together in an integrated plan; and evaluate the design's overall effectiveness, cost, reliability, and safety. This process applies to products as different as chemicals, computers, gas turbines, helicopters, and toys.

In addition to design and development, many engineers work in testing, production, or maintenance. Here they may supervise production in factories, determine the causes of breakdowns, and test manufactured products to maintain quality. They also estimate the time and cost to complete projects.

Engineers often use computers to simulate and test how a machine, structure, or system operates. Many engineers also use computer-aided design systems to produce and analyze designs. They spend a great deal of time writing reports and consulting with other engineers, as complex projects often require an interdisciplinary team of engineers. Supervisory engineers are responsible for major components or entire projects.

Most engineers specialize. More than twenty-five major specialties are recognized by professional societies, and within the major branches are numerous subdivisions. Structural, environmental, and transportation engineering, for example, are subdivisions of civil engineering. Engineers also may specialize in one industry, such as motor vehicles, or in one field of technology, such as propulsion or guidance systems.

Qualifications and Training

A bachelor's degree in engineering from an accredited engineering program is usually required for beginning engineering jobs. College graduates with a degree in a physical science or mathematics may occasionally qualify for some engineering jobs, especially in engineering specialties in high demand at the time. Most engineering degrees are granted in branches such as electrical, mechanical, or civil engineering. However, engineers trained in one branch may work in another. This flexibility allows employers to meet staffing needs in new technologies and specialties where engineers are in short supply. It also allows engineers to shift to fields with better employment prospects or to ones that match their interests more closely.

In addition to the standard engineering degree, many colleges offer degrees in engineering technology, which are offered as either two- or four-year sequences. These programs prepare students for practical design and production work rather than for jobs that require more theoretical, scientific, and mathematical knowledge. Graduates of four-year technology programs may get jobs similar to those obtained by graduates with a bachelor's degree in engineering. Some employers regard them as having skills between those of a technician and an engineer.

Graduate training is essential for engineering faculty positions but is not required for the majority of entry-level engineering jobs. Many engineers obtain graduate degrees in engineering or business administration to learn new technology, broaden their education, and enhance promotion opportunities; others obtain law degrees and become attorneys. Many high-level executives in government and industry began their careers as engineers.

A large number of colleges and universities offer a bachelor's degree in engineering. Many offer a bachelor's degree in engineering technology, although not all are accredited programs. (Be sure to check this out before enrolling!) Although most institutions offer programs in the larger branches of engineering, only a few offer some of the smaller specialties. Also, programs of the same title may vary in content. For example, some emphasize industrial practices, preparing students for jobs in industry, while others are more theoretical and are better for students preparing to take graduate work. Therefore, students should investigate curricula and check accreditations carefully before selecting a college.

Bachelor's degree programs in engineering are typically designed to last four years, but many students find that it takes between four and five years to complete their studies. In a typical four-year college curriculum, the first two years are spent studying basic sciences (mathematics, physics, and chemistry), introductory engineering, and the humanities, social sciences, and English. In the last two years, most courses are in engineering, usually with a concentration in one branch. For example, the last two years of an aerospace program might include courses such as fluid mechanics, heat transfer, applied aerodynamics, analytical mechanics, flight vehicle design, trajectory dynamics, and aerospace propulsion systems.

All fifty states and the District of Columbia require registration for engineers whose work may affect life, health, or property, or who offer their services to the public. Registration generally requires a degree from an engineering program accredited by the Accreditation Board for Engineering and Technology, four years of relevant work experience, and successful completion of a state examination. Some states will not register people with degrees in engineering technology.

Beginning engineering graduates usually do routine work under the supervision of experienced engineers and, in larger companies, may also receive formal classroom or seminar-type training. As they gain knowledge and experience, they are assigned more difficult tasks with greater independence to develop designs, solve problems, and make decisions.

Engineers should be able to work as part of a team and should be creative, analytical, and detail oriented. In addition, engineers should be able to communicate well—both orally and in writing.

Professionals in this field must realize that continued education is vitally important throughout their careers because much of their value to their employer depends on their knowledge of the latest technology. The pace of technological change varies by engineering specialty and industry. Engineers in high-technology areas such as advanced electronics may find that technical knowledge can become obsolete rapidly. Even those who continue to pursue education are vulnerable if the particular technology or product they have specialized in becomes obsolete. Engineers who have not kept current in their fields may find themselves passed over for promotions and are vulnerable should layoffs occur. On the other hand, it is often these high-technology areas that offer the greatest challenges, the most interesting work, and the highest salaries. Therefore, the choice of engineering specialty and employer involves an assessment not only of the potential rewards but also of the risk of technological obsolescence.

Salaries

Below is a list of average yearly salaries for some engineering specialties:

Metallurgists and Metallurgical, Ceramic, and Materials Engineers	$57,000
Mining Engineers	$54,970
Petroleum Engineers	$70,090
Chemical Engineers	$61,240

Nuclear Engineers	$68,020
Civil Engineers	$54,660
Agricultural Engineers	$53,710
Electrical and Electronic Engineers	$59,670
Computer Engineers	$59,850
Industrial Engineers	$54,450
Safety Engineers	$53,170
Mechanical Engineers	$54,550
All Other Engineers	$59,160

Meet and Greet

Mary Shafer

Mary Shafer is a NASA senior aerospace engineer at the premier installation for aeronautical flight research—the Dryden Flight Research Center. Located in the Mojave Desert at Edward's Air Force Base in California, the center celebrated its fiftieth anniversary in 1996. Dryden has grown from an initial group of five engineers to a facility with more than 460 NASA government employees and about the same number of civilian contract personnel. In addition to carrying out aeronautical research, the center also supports the space shuttle program as a primary and backup landing site and as a facility to test and validate design concepts and systems used in development and operation.

"As a high school senior in the early sixties, I attended a National Science Foundation course at UCLA between my junior and senior years," Shafer says. "The subject happened to be meteorology, but it gave me a chance to see that science and research provided a way to explain the world around me, which I felt was interesting and important. Then I got a summer job working for the U.S. Air Force, where I discovered I liked being near airplanes.

"I began my college career at UCLA as a chemistry major but later switched to engineering, spending subsequent summers working for NASA. I decided I truly wanted to focus my career on airplanes and flight research and was lucky in my quest. I encountered a number of exceptional people who were willing to educate me about aerodynamics and fluid mechanics.

"During the summers at NASA, I began by reducing data, working with a ruler in engineering units, plotting the information on graph paper with orange carbon behind it. I wrote a couple of smaller programs that impressed everybody (because at that point few people could do that). The next year, I progressed to writing computer matrix manipulations designed to measure trial-time stability analysis during flight. That was really interesting because I started to understand the rules that govern how airplanes fly.

"I earned my bachelor's degree and came back and worked another summer writing quality programs for some of the engineers. Then I went back and got my master's degree. The next summer, I was writing with engineers and even married one!

"I began working as a computer programmer writing follow-up programs for the X-24B, then worked for Lockheed on the Federal Aviation Administration certification of the L-1011. I moved on to McDonald Douglas and McDonald Aircraft, then worked on the F-4 airplane and the initial acceptance testing of the F-15. Then I accepted a position in the air force as a systems designer working on writing programs. Finally, I came back over to NASA and got a job as a controls engineer.

"My projects vary, but right now, in addition to a number of small flying-qualities research projects, I'm working on one particular experiment called the aerospy. It is my responsibility to look at an airplane's various flying qualities to make sure that any modifications that are made are safe. We must fulfill our priority of being able to fly airplanes that are structurally sound.

"Most of my day is spent either talking with pilots, studying data on various computers, visiting the simulation area to see how the plane is flying, watching the input of our new ideas, or observing what the airplane looks like with the new lift, drag, or whatever the case may be. Then we put the results of our efforts in the simulator so that the pilots can fly the planes and determine if the real planes will fly as we want them to. For example, we focus on issues such as: Are we going to have enough runway to take off? Are we going to have enough thrust? Will it go forward instead of falling out of the sky?

"My other real interest lies in how the aircraft pilot system works and what the pilot needs to get from the airplane in order to feel that it's a good airplane or a bad airplane. In his opening sentence in Anna Karenina, Tolstoy says 'All happy families are alike, but each unhappy family is unhappy in its own way.' Well, the same is true of airplanes—a good airplane is not very interesting to a quality engineer, but a bad airplane is fascinating.

"I work fairly regular hours. However, it's my understanding that this is somewhat less common in the university setting. The situation here is that we'll occasionally have a surge of work. For instance, I've got to write a paper that is due in three months, so I'll probably do that on weekends but then go back to a normal work schedule.

"NASA employs aeronautical engineers, mechanical engineers, electrical engineers, meteorologists, and physicists. We cover a broad range of disciplines: engineering and the hard sciences, chemistry, physics, meteorology, and math. It's important that you know math and extremely important that you know how to program and use the computer. Also, you need to know how to write with clarity and grammatical precision. There's no point in doing research if you can't write it down clearly and well enough that people can understand what you did, how you did it, why you did it, and what happened when you did it.

"Flexibility is another important quality for researchers because you don't know how your attempts are going to come out and you have to be able to build upon your successes or shift gears when the outcome isn't as you planned. People who are unable to deal with uncertainty may find that research is not a good field for them. And in this line of work, a robust ego is a nice thing to have.

"Research is essentially a mutual endeavor. When you begin a project, you never really know what will be gained from your efforts, what will be gleaned, or how the new information might be used. It is only in the later stages of your work that you may be able to ascertain exactly how the information gained from your research will affect others on a grander scale. This is what provides fulfillment for all scientists and engineers—uncovering or discovering information that can benefit the world in which we all live."

Ernestine Meyers

Ernestine Meyers serves as senior environmental engineer for the Division of Sanitation Facilities Construction in the Office of Environmental Health and Engineering of the United States Public Health Service in Albuquerque, New Mexico.

"While I was growing up, my summers were spent out in the field with my father," Meyers explains. "That's how I became familiar with the inner workings of the Indian Health Service. He worked for the agency as an environmental health technician for thirty-two years. Together we would travel to different reservations where I would observe what he did. I met and talked with engineers and got to know what they were responsible for. And, of course, I helped whenever I could. With my father as a role model and my love for science and the outdoors, I found my career direction.

"Born on a New Mexico Pueblo reservation, I am the oldest of four children. Given my choice to attend the Bureau of Indian

Affairs (BIA) school or a public school in a nearby town, I decided to attend public school a few miles from the pueblo. Each day I traveled to school on a bus driven by my grandfather. Some of my friends went to BIA schools, and some went to public schools. My father attended public school, and my mother had gone to BIA. I was able to make my own choice as long as I took learning seriously. In my family, education was strongly stressed. My mother is a nurse, my uncle is an educator, another uncle is a surgeon, and many members of my extended family had gone on to earn college degrees.

"As the oldest, I was strongly urged to continue my education, so I embarked on a program that would include all the college preparatory classes I would need to ensure my entrance into a college or university. Even at the high school level, I enjoyed science and knew that would be my field of concentration.

"During the summer of my junior year in high school, I attended the Minority Introduction to Engineering course at New Mexico State University. I was exposed to all the different types of engineering. Civil engineering easily became my choice because I always loved the outdoors. I knew I wouldn't be happy sitting at a desk or computer all the time.

"After high school, I enrolled at New Mexico State, since I had received a positive introduction to its engineering program. In addition, my uncle worked there, I had friends going to school there, and it was my home state. Happily, I was awarded a four-year scholarship from the U.S. Health Service. Thus, I became a freshman there in the fall of 1979. The scholarship paid for all my undergraduate education, but in return I was obligated to work for the agency for four years following my graduation.

"After receiving my bachelor of science degree in environmental engineering, I was assigned to the city of Tuba, Arizona, on a Navajo Indian reservation. As a field engineer, I was responsible for planning and organizing the construction of sanitation facilities and bringing in water lines for individual families. I found it to be very rewarding work, and it seems that the Navajos agreed. When I left, they presented me with an achievement medal for the work I did during those four years.

"A typical day consists of working on the plans and designs for a pueblo springhouse, spending time with the surveyors who are doing the groundwork for some of my projects, working on specifications or proposals for future projects, dealing with contractors, or helping out the other engineers when they have any technical questions.

"Another of my focuses is my membership in the Commission Corps of the Public Health Service, one of the branches of the military. We have uniforms just like the navy. Upon finishing my bachelor of science degree, I had a choice of entering as a civil service employee or applying for the Commission Corps. I elected to apply for the Commission Corps because I was told that I would probably advance more quickly that way. Today I hold the rank of lieutenant commander.

"In August of 1988, I transferred to the Pacific Northwest and worked with three different tribes, assuming the same duties as I had previously. I was the only field engineer in the office, and it was kind of scary at first, but I learned to be independent. In 1991, I was selected engineer of the year for the Portland area.

"After three years, the Indian Health Service chose me to attend long-term training to get my master's degree in environmental engineering. The offer allowed me to go to school for one year and still receive my regular yearly salary. All educational expenses were absorbed by the agency. I felt that this was such a wonderful offer, I could not turn it down.

"I returned to New Mexico State for my advanced degree. The only hard part is that you must finish in one year, and the program is really a two-year program. It's pretty difficult to keep up, but if you are dedicated to accomplishing something, you will succeed. It may not be easy, but nothing that's worth accomplishing ever is. Every time you reach a goal you've set for yourself, it's time to set another. You should always do the best you can. Just meeting minimum standards is not good enough."

Albert L. de Richemond

Albert L. de Richemond is associate director of Health Devices Group at ECRI of Plymouth Meeting, Pennsylvania. He earned his bachelor of science degree from Penn State, his master of science degree from Virginia Tech, and did post-master's work at Drexel University in Philadelphia. Following this, he received his Pennsylvania professional engineer's license in 1983.

"I thought about becoming an engineer in high school," says de Richemond. "At that time, the SATs provided some guidance on what careers best suited a person—according to scores on the test. I just missed the score that pointed to medicine. Engineering was indicated for me and was supported by my outside school interests (taking things apart to find out how they worked, building things, backyard experiments, reading about science, and working in power plants and refineries).

"I chose my particular specialty after hearing about it in my freshman year. It was presented as being the foundation of most of the other engineering disciplines and as providing a broad education. It is and did. It is also mathematically oriented and offers a way of thinking about the world and how it works.

"In graduate school, I took many additional courses that enabled me to apply for medical school, but that did not work out. However, medicine still remained an area of interest. In graduate school, I started out in biomechanical engineering, but my professor became critically ill, and the program was abolished. So I became a graduate teaching assistant, a position that I found to be most enjoyable.

"Subsequently, I worked for GE Re-Entry Systems Division and for two midsize companies that make heavy processing equipment. I enjoyed this field because I was able to experiment, to get into the field where our equipment was used, to get into the factories where we built the equipment, and to solve problems with the designs.

"During my tenure at these companies, I studied for and passed the professional engineer's exam and became licensed in

Pennsylvania. This was a validation for me. I felt that it showed both me and the world that I was a capable engineer.

"Following this, I hired on with a small company as a research designer. I enjoyed setting up a prototype lab and working with relatively new computer analysis programs. Then I moved to my present organization as an evaluation engineer for a special project. Completion of this led to moving within the organization to the medical device evaluation group. This position truly unites my two areas of interest—engineering and medicine. During the forty hours of my workweek, I now deal with clinicians and manufacturers and help them solve problems through engineering.

"My job involves talking with people (subscribers, employees, managers, visitors), examining things (medical devices, computer problems, situations), interpreting information (standards, published articles), reading (draft articles for our journals and periodicals, pertinent articles), writing (articles for our journal, new standards, reports), and making decisions (what to write about, how to test something, why something happened). On a typical day, I'll spend a few minutes on many topics, bouncing from one to another as the need arises due to E-mail, office visits from coworkers, meetings, telephone calls, more information, discussions, and so forth. I am always busy even without appearing busy because I am continually thinking about the various things I am doing or have yet to do. Sometimes the work is very relaxed, but other times it can be quite tense due to the importance of the event (deposition, personnel issue). There is also the risk of catching a disease from contaminated equipment received for accident investigation.

"Our environment is casual and friendly. Most everyone has his or her own office, and none of the offices have doors. Anyone can ask anyone else for information or help at any time. We all have beepers, and the building has telephones everywhere, so we can be in instant contact should a customer need our expertise. Most of us have 24-7 access to the building and do come in after normal hours to do some odd jobs.

"The best aspects of my job involve the variety of work, the ability to help others and have a positive effect on something, and the people I work with—who are all very intelligent and capable.

"I would recommend that others who are interested in this field read voraciously and widely. Go to college and learn how to think. Pick a subject and study it, but don't expect to use all of it in the workaday world. Be a generalist. Learn how to multitask. Figure out how to control stress. Become flexible in thinking and in body. Learn about people and how they operate. And last but not least—learn how to balance the important things in your life."

For Additional Information

American Society for Engineering Education
1818 N Street NW, Suite 1600
Washington, DC 20036
www.asee.org

Junior Engineering Technical Society
1420 King Street, Suite 405
Alexandria, VA 22314
www.jets.org

American Institute of Aeronautics and Astronautics, Inc.
1801 Alexander Bell Drive, Suite 500
Reston, VA 20191
www.aiaa.org

American Institute of Chemical Engineers
345 East Forty-Seventh Street
New York, NY 10017
www.aiche.org

American Chemical Society
Department of Career Services
1155 Sixteenth Street NW
Washington, DC 20036
www.acs.org

American Society of Civil Engineers
1801 Alexander Bell Drive
Reston, VA 20191
www.asce.org

Institute of Electrical and Electronics Engineers
1828 L Street NW, Suite 1202
Washington, DC 20036
www.ieee.org

Institute of Industrial Engineers, Inc.,
25 Technology Park
Norcross, GA 30092
www.iienet.org

The American Society of Mechanical Engineers
345 East Forty-Seventh Street
New York, NY 10017
www.asme.org

The Minerals, Metals, & Materials Society
420 Commonwealth Drive
Warrendale, PA 15086
www.tms.org

ASM International
Student Outreach Program
Materials Park, OH 44073
www.asm.com

The Society for Mining, Metallurgy, and Exploration, Inc.
P.O. Box 625002
Littleton, CO 80162
www.smenet.org

American Nuclear Society
555 North Kensington Avenue
LaGrange Park, IL 60525
www.ans.org

Society of Petroleum Engineers
P.O. Box 833836
Richardson, TX 75083
www.spe.org

CHAPTER FIVE

Careers in Medicine

He is the best physician who is the most ingenious inspirer of hope.
SAMUEL TAYLOR COLERIDGE

Help Wanted: Board-Certified Internist

We are seeking a board-certified internist for a hospital position in Salt Lake City, Utah. The physician will practice with an established inpatient management group serving a well-known, quality medical group. Physician's duties will include managing adults in the hospital from admission through the acute phase of illness to discharge.

Please contact our national director of recruitment to find out more about this important position.

Solving Puzzles in Medicine

As one of the most prestigious and fulfilling professions, medicine truly epitomizes both the science and the art of puzzle solving. An individual goes to the doctor because he or she doesn't feel right. The doctor can only provide relief for the patient if he or she manages to figure out the puzzle—what is it that is causing these symptoms? What is the right approach to alleviating the distress? If you are attracted to solving these kinds of puzzles, making a difference in your world, and serving others, then this chapter on doctors may indeed be valuable!

Zeroing In on What a Doctor Does

There are two general categories that physicians fall into—the M.D. (Doctor of Medicine) and the D.O. (Doctor of Osteopathic Medicine). M.D.s are also known as osteopathic physicians. While M.D.s and D.O.s may use all accepted methods of treatment, D.O.s put special emphasis on holistic care, preventive medicine, and the body's musculoskeletal system.

Primary care physicians, including those who focus on general and family medicine, general internal medicine, or general pediatrics, account for about one-third of all M.D.s. When we get sick (or, perhaps more importantly, want to stay well), we consult these professionals first, as they are trained to provide a wide range of services that children and adults need. Thus, primary care doctors commonly see the same patients again and again.

General and family practitioners emphasize comprehensive health care for patients of all ages and for the family as a whole. *General internists* provide care mainly for adults who have a wide range of problems associated with the body's organs. *General pediatricians* are charged with children's health.

Specialists

When deemed necessary, primary care physicians refer patients to specialists. Specialist physicians are different from generalists in that they focus on treating a particular system or part of the body. Some of the experts in this category include *ophthalmologists*, who specialize in the eye; *cardiologists*, who focus on the heart; and *neurologists*, who study the brain. Working together, the generalists and specialists make sure that patients receive the care that they need for specific medical problems and sustained health throughout their lives.

The American Medical Association reports the following breakdown of doctors and their specialties:

General internal medicine	16.0%
Unspecified/unknown/inactive	14.4%
General and family medicine	10.0%
General pediatrics	7.0%
Psychiatry	5.3%
General surgery	5.2%
Obstetrics and gynecology	5.2%
Anesthesiology	4.6%
Orthopedic surgery	3.1%
Diagnostic radiology	2.7%
Emergency medicine	2.7%
Cardiovascular diseases	2.6%
Pathology	2.5%
Ophthalmology	2.4%
Neurology	1.6%
Urological surgery	1.4%
Gastroenterology	1.3%
Otolaryngology	1.3%
Dermatology	1.2%
Radiology	1.1%
Other specialties	1.0%
Pulmonary diseases	1.0%
Child psychiatry	.8%
Physical medicine and rehabilitation	.8%

Plastic surgery	.8%
Neurological surgery	.7%
Allergy	.5%
Radiation oncology	.5%
Occupational medicine	.4%
Thoracic surgery	.3%
General preventive medicine	.2%
Nuclear medicine	.2%
Pediatric cardiology	.2%
Public health	.2%
Aerospace medicine	.1%
Colon and rectal surgery	.1%
Forensic pathology	.1%

On the Job

A career as a doctor is hardly an easy one. Besides the obvious, excessive strain of having to make difficult, perhaps life-and-death decisions, physicians may be required to work long days. Early morning and evening hours are often a necessity. However, in recent years there has been a shift. Physicians are increasingly practicing in groups or health care organizations that provide backup coverage and allow for some time off. Since these physicians often work as part of a group, they are able to take more personal time off than the earlier doctors who operated as sole practitioners.

Physicians are often required to travel from office to hospitals in order to treat their patients. They may also be called in for emergency situations. And even when they are not seeing patients, they may spend a good part of their time advising individuals who call with various medical concerns and complaints. About 70 percent of all doctors work out of an office (including HMOs and clinics). About another 20 percent are employed by hospitals; the rest practice in the federal government—most in the Department of Veterans Affairs hospitals and clinics or in the Public Health Service of the Department of Health and Human Services.

The Northeastern and Western states have the highest ratio of physicians to population; the South Central states have the lowest. D.O.s are more likely than M.D.s to practice in small cities and in towns and in rural areas. M.D.s tend to locate in urban areas close to hospital and educational centers.

Overwhelmingly, osteopathic physicians make their homes in states that have osteopathic schools and hospitals. In a recent survey, about one-half of them were found to be practicing in six states: New Jersey, Ohio, Pennsylvania, Michigan, Florida, and Texas.

Qualifications and Training

If you are considering medicine as a profession, it is important that you realize that becoming a doctor is a very arduous process that requires many, many years of formal study.

As a rule, you will need to spend four years in undergraduate school, four years in medical school, and three to eight years in your chosen specialty's internship and residency. In some instances, medical schools offer a combined undergraduate and medical school program that lasts six years instead of the usual eight years.

Premedical students must complete undergraduate work in physics, biology, mathematics, English, organic and inorganic chemistry, the social sciences, and humanities. Additionally, many often volunteer at local medical facilities in order to get a step ahead and gain some valuable practical experience.

The minimum educational requirement for entry to a medical or osteopathic school is three years of college. (However, most applicants have at least a bachelor's degree. Indeed, many have advanced degrees.)

A large number of students apply to medical school at the closing of their junior year in college and then begin medical study after graduation. In other cases, prospective doctors complete their college work and then enter the labor force for a number of years before they begin their medical training. Still others decide to opt for early admission or other similar programs that allow students (who have shown a high level of academic achievement and maturity) to proceed to their medical education at a more accelerated rate.

Successfully Entering Medical School

Warning—gaining acceptance into medical school is difficult. Only about one-third who apply are invited to enter. In addition to your undergraduate work, most schools also require you to take the Medical College Admission Test (MCAT), which is intended to evaluate your knowledge of the basic sciences, reading and writing aptitudes, and problem-solving capabilities.

One plus is that applying to medical school has been made considerably easier thanks to the American Medical College Application Service (AMCAS). Most medical schools (about 113) participate in this program. To apply, all you need to do is fill out one application and send it, along with your official transcripts, to AMCAS. Once the information you provided is verified, this service will distribute your application to all of the schools you have designated. If you are interested in a school that

3802688

does not participate in this plan, just contact the admissions office of the school directly.

When you are being considered for admission, you will be judged by the courses you completed, your college grades, personal qualities, letters of recommendation, your MCAT scores, extracurricular activities, and interviews with medical school admissions committees (held late in the application process). Other elements may include leadership qualities, strength of character, and personality.

Medical School and Beyond

While in medical school, a lot will be expected of you—both in terms of the volume you will be expected to master and the rate necessary to keep up. To accomplish this, you will need solid study habits and strong time-management skills. The good news is that a very high percentage of students who are accepted to medical school do manage to complete all of the necessary study and requirements to obtain an M.D. degree.

Most of the first two years of a medical student's life is spent in laboratories and classrooms taking courses such as anatomy, biochemistry, physiology, pharmacology, psychology, microbiology, pathology, medical ethics, and laws governing medicine. Prospective physicians also learn how to take medical histories, examine patients, and diagnose illnesses.

During the last two years, students work with patients under the supervision of experienced physicians in hospitals and clinics. Through rotations in internal medicine, family practice, obstetrics and gynecology, pediatrics, psychiatry, and surgery, medical students gain valuable experience in the diagnosis and treatment of illness.

Following medical school, almost all M.D.s enter a residency-graduate program of medical education in a specialty that takes the form of paid on-the-job training, usually at a hospital. Following graduation, most D.O.s serve a twelve-month rotating internship. Then they enter residencies that may last two to six years. Residencies in managed care settings may be a distinct advantage, since these programs provide experience with this increasingly common type of medical practice.

Licensing for Physicians

All states, plus the District of Columbia and U.S. territories, require mandatory licensing for physicians before they can begin to serve as doctors. To be licensed, physicians must graduate from an accredited medical school, pass a licensing examination, and complete one to seven years of graduate medical education. Although physicians licensed in one state can usually get a license to practice in another without future examination, some states limit reciprocity. Graduates of foreign medical schools can qualify for a license after passing an examination and completing a U.S. residency.

Physicians who wish to specialize are required to engage in additional training. Depending on the specialty, M.D.s and D.O.s (seeking board certification in a specialty) may spend up to an additional seven years. A final examination immediately after residency, or after one or two years of practice, is also necessary for board certification by the American Board of Medical Specialists (ABMS) or the American Osteopathic Association (AOA). There are twenty-four specialty boards, ranging from allergy and immunology to urology. For certification in a subspecialty, physicians usually need another one to two years of residency.

On a personal level, individuals who wish to become physicians must have a desire to serve patients, be self-motivated, and be able to survive the pressures and long hours of medical education and practice. Physicians must also have a good bedside manner, emotional stability, and the ability to make decisions in emergencies.

Becoming a doctor is draining in another area too—finances. And while the cost of education has increased, student financial assistance has not. As a result, more than 80 percent of medical students need to borrow money to cover their expenses.

Salaries

Earnings for physicians are among the highest for any occupation. According to the American Medical Association, median income, after expenses, for osteopathic physicians is about $164,000. The middle 50 percent earn between $120,000 and $250,000.

The American Medical Association offers the following yearly figures:

Radiology	$260,000
Anesthesiology	$220,000
Surgery	$217,000
Obstetrics/gynecology	$200,000
Emergency medicine	$195,000
Pathology	$175,000
General internal medicine	$147,000
General/family practice	$132,000
Psychiatry	$130,000
Pediatrics	$120,000

Self-employed physicians—those who own or are part owners of a medical practice—have higher median incomes than salaried physicians. Earnings vary according to the number of years in practice, geographic region, hours worked, and skill, personality, and professional reputation. According to the Association of American Medical Colleges, the average salary of medical residents ranges from about $34,100 (for first-year residents) to about $42,100 (for those in the sixth year).

Meet and Greet

Lawrence C. Newman, M.D.

Lawrence C. Newman is the director of the Headache Institute at St. Luke's–Roosevelt Hospital Center in New York. He received his B.A. in biology from Clark University in Worcester, Massachusetts, in 1979 and his M.D. from the Universidad Autonoma de Guadalajara, Mexico, in 1983. He completed his residency in internal medicine at Elmhurst Hospital Center in Queens, New York; a residency in neurology at Albert Einstein College of Medicine in the Bronx, New York; served as chief resident in neurology at Albert Einstein College of Medicine in the Bronx and received a Headache Fellowship at Montefiore Medical Center in the Bronx.

"I knew that I would be a doctor from the age of five or six," says Dr. Newman. "For one thing, I thought that my pediatrician was a wonderful person. I used to make gifts for him in school and actually looked forward to office visits. In fact, while I was in college, I spent my summers doing research in his lab.

"My great-uncle Nat was also an inspiration to me. He was, and probably still is, the best physician I have ever met. He was a fantastic diagnostician, had a wonderful bedside manner, and was a true gentleman. Upon his retirement, his patients all got together and organized a surprise party for him to show their appreciation. One of my biggest thrills was having my uncle attend one of my lectures—and remark that he actually learned something!

"Originally, I thought that I was going to become a pediatrician. And throughout medical school, I still maintained that belief. During my training, however, I learned a lot about myself. I found that, while I enjoyed treating children and interacting with them while they were healthy, I had a very hard time treating youngsters who were very ill. Many nights I would come home and cry. I realized I could not do this for the rest of my life.

"I also discovered that the field of neurology was fascinating. The different parts of the nervous system—the brain, spinal cord, and peripheral nerves—made up a complicated network. Determining where the problem lay was like figuring out a puzzle—I could tell exactly what part was injured by closely examining the patient.

"Headaches have always held a special attraction for me. Patients with headaches are usually young and otherwise totally healthy. Nonetheless, their lives have been totally disrupted by these painful attacks, as have the lives of those around them—their families, friends, neighbors, and coworkers. Added to this, most patients with headaches are not properly treated by their physicians and are often misunderstood and left to suffer needlessly. Trying to figure out what type of headache the patient has is a challenge that I really enjoy. Since there are about three hundred medical conditions that have headache as a symptom, it can be challenging. Trying to determine the correct treatment—not everything works for everybody with the same condition—is also an intriguing aspect of my profession. But the greatest part is helping to stop people's suffering so they can get back to their lives.

"My job has many different parts—some of them are more enjoyable than others. For me, the best parts of my career involve taking care of patients.

"Here is my regular routine during the four days a week that I see patients in my office from ten in the morning until five in the afternoon. I take a history first and ask a lot of questions about headaches and other health-related issues. Following this, I perform an examination and then set up a treatment plan to help minimize the attacks and also to treat attacks when they occur.

"I also have rooms in my office to treat patients who develop pain at home and don't get relief from the medications they are taking. I can treat them with injectable medications or even set up an intravenous treatment.

"I am also involved in clinical trials in which I test new, promising medications before they are approved for use. These studies help to prove whether these medications work well and show whether they are safe.

"Another part of my job that I really like is education. With medical students, doctors in training, and practicing doctors in attendance, I frequently lecture about the newest and best ways to treat headache patients. I also get to write book chapters and journal articles about the work I have been doing and to present the findings of my work at medical conferences throughout the world.

"Sometimes the work is stressful—especially on the days when the patients aren't doing well. There are a lot of telephone calls to answer, even after the office closes, because people can get sick anytime—daytime, nighttime, even holidays.

"Though I don't enjoy the very long hours that often don't leave me enough time to spend with my family, there is no job I prefer. I have never had any regrets. Though the hours are long, the work is stressful, and the training needed to be a doctor takes so many years (four years of college, four years of medical school, and then five years of training), I would do it all again. Being a physician is everything I imagined it would be when I was a kid looking up to my pediatrician and my uncle.

"My advice to others would be to never give up. If one path doesn't work, always try new avenues. In my case, so many people were trying to get into medical school when I applied, the opportunities just weren't there. So I sought my education outside of the country. Many of my friends gave up and went into business. That would definitely have been a mistake for me. So I would tell others to just keep working toward your goal."

Robert S. Gotlin, M.D.

Robert S. Gotlin is the director of orthopedic and sports rehabilitation in the Department of Orthopedic Surgery at Beth Israel Medical Center in New York. He earned a bachelor of science degree from the State University of New York and then attended the National College of Chiropractic in Illinois and Southeastern University of the Health Sciences in Miami. He is also an assistant professor of rehabilitation at the Albert Einstein College of Medicine at Yeshiva University.

"A passion for helping others and the joy of a respected career are the two main reasons that I chose medicine," says Dr. Gotlin. "Since I had a strong passion for exercise and fitness, it was logical for me to choose orthopedic and sports medicine as my specialty track.

"As a practicing physician, keeping busy and being creative are the two things that fuel my day. What keeps me going is the grateful look on someone's face when they are relieved of pain or free from the weakness that brought them to see me. Since medicine includes both art and science, the ability to be creative and dynamic is inherent in this kind of work. Change is the nature of the beast, so one must be open-minded and always ready for new ideas and methods for treatment. When you serve as a physician, I feel that mastering your interpersonal skills cannot be overstated as a foundation for success. No two people are alike, and each person must be treated as an individual.

"The typical day for me is lengthy and extensive, starting at 5:30 A.M. and ending when I just can't function any longer. Patient care, research, literature reviews, and practice management are intimately integrated with my family duties, including coaching seven youth sports teams and extensive community youth sports development commitments. Still, all of this brings a smile to my face.

"Dedicating your career to helping others can be a most gratifying experience—and one that can be accomplished via many avenues. For me, medicine is the vehicle for traveling the avenue of helping those in need. Caring for a health-conscious population through orthopedic medicine and sports rehabilitation enables me to not only treat ailments but also to educate, guide, and influence people's everyday lifestyles in a positive way.

"Whatever career you might choose, it is easier to successfully accomplish your goals when you have a passion for that particular field. So many times during life, obstacles alter the direction you are traveling, and if the glass of water on the table is viewed as 'half full' rather than 'half empty,' achieving your goals is more likely. I strongly urge any individual to learn about and experience firsthand the day-to-day demands for your chosen field. Then ask yourself, 'Where will I be and what will I be doing ten years from now?' If there is any uncertainly, rethink your career choice. If there is certainty and a real passion for that career, the answer to this question will easily be answered. To this day, fifteen years into my career, my passion is as strong as ever, and my drive into work each day is still something I look forward to."

For Additional Information

Association of American Medical Colleges
Section for Student Services
2450 N Street NW
Washington, DC 20037
www.aamc.org

American Medical Association
Department of Communications and Public Relations
515 North State Street
Chicago, IL 60610
www.ama-assn.org

American Osteopathic Association
Department of Public Relations
142 East Ontario Street
Chicago, IL 60611
www.aoa-net.org

American Association of Colleges of Osteopathic Medicine
5550 Friendship Boulevard, Suite 310
Chevy Chase, MD 20815
www.aacom.org

American Academy of Family Physicians
11400 Tomahawk Creek Parkway
Leawood, KS 66211
www.aafp.org

American Academy of Pediatrics
National Headquarters
141 Northwest Point Boulevard
Elk Grove Village, IL 60007
www.aap.org

American Academy of Pediatrics
Department of Federal Affairs
601 Thirteenth Street NW
Suite 400 North
Washington, DC 20005
www.aap.org

American College of Physicians
Independence Mall West
Sixth Street at Race
Philadelphia, PA 19106
www.acponline.org

CHAPTER SIX

Careers in Automobile Mechanics

Hard work spotlights the character of people: some turn up their sleeves, some turn up their noses, and some don't turn up at all.
SAM EWIG

Help Wanted: Automobile Mechanic

If you want to have the best opportunity for your career and your family, please contact us immediately! We have immediate openings for auto service technicians in your area.

Whether you are a seasoned veteran or just looking to gain auto experience, we want to hear from you. We offer top pay and benefits, including health insurance, a retirement program, and much more. The more ASE certifications and experience you have, the higher the pay.

Zeroing In on What an Auto Mechanic Does

Did you spend your childhood playing with die-cast cars and perfecting your *vroom, vroom* noises? Did you then move on to meticulously assembling model cars using hundreds of tiny pieces? As you neared driving age, did dreaming about (and saving for) your first car consume your every waking moment? If you're interested in a career as an auto mechanic, chances are you've been captivated with cars, and everything about them, for as long as you can remember.

Auto mechanics, also called automotive service technicians, repair and maintain cars and light trucks. A mechanic may work on all parts of the car or may choose to specialize in certain parts (transmissions, brakes) or on certain makes, models, or classes (Cadillacs, Fords, foreign sports cars).

The most challenging part of the job—and the most enjoyable for many—is the diagnosis itself. Finding the problem quickly requires skill, experience, and good reasoning abilities on the part of the mechanic. Computers are being used more and more to help diagnose malfunctions, but many problems are still found the old-fashioned, hands-on way.

Because mechanics must examine the vehicle, figure out the problem, then treat or fix the problem accordingly, they could be compared to physicians. Both professions deal with people who wait until they're desperate to seek advice, often when regular preventive maintenance could possibly have avoided the problem altogether. Once the problem is diagnosed and dealt with, both professions then counsel on the benefits of regular checkups and tune-ups.

Mechanics and doctors must also keep up with changing technology and treatment methods, but let's face it: the human body has been functioning in essentially the same way for thousands of years. Cars and all their components, however, are often radically different from model to model, and they are constantly being improved and changed by their makers. In this way, being an auto mechanic can actually be even more difficult than being a doctor.

Good mechanics must be continually aware of the potential hazards and dangers associated with the job. Safety standards regulate a mechanic's exposure to loud noise, fumes, odors, and hazardous liquids, but these factors are usually present nonetheless. Mechanics must also work with very dirty and greasy parts and often in very awkward (and sometimes painful) positions. Cuts, bruises, and burns are not uncommon. Mechanics must also be able to lift heavy parts and tools, and, of course, there's always risk associated with being underneath a car, whether it's being hydraulically lifted or resting on all four tires. Additionally, mechanics must be prepared to work long hours on Saturday, since that is often a repair shop's busiest day.

If you're fascinated with cars but don't relish the idea of ever-present grease on your hands, you might also consider a career in auto body repair or automotive detailing, or an even "cleaner" venture such as auto sales at a dealership or serving as a repair shop's service writer or estimator.

Qualifications and Training

Training can begin as early as high school, because many high schools offer vocational classes in automotive mechanics and electrical trades. Candidates should also take as many classes as possible in math and physical science. High school is also a good time to begin filling the toolbox. Employers will usually provide the larger, more expensive tools, but mechanics are usually required to have their own extensive inventory of most of the tools they'll need to do the job.

After high school, those wishing to pursue a career in auto mechanics complete an automotive technology program offered by a community college, technical school, or vocational school. These schools usually work with local repair shops to get internships for their students while they're in the program.

To become certified, mechanics must spend more than a thousand hours working on cars, then pass a written exam. Such certification is not required by law but is usually required by employers. Some shops also require union membership.

Once on the job, mechanics must continue training in order to keep up with the changing technology. This can be done formally, through seminars and classes, or more informally, by simply poring over updated service manuals.

Aside from formal training, successful mechanics must be able to read and write well, have good hearing and eyesight, and possess a certain degree of mechanical aptitude and manual dexterity. They must be skilled with an ever-changing array of hand tools and power tools, both common ones and those made specifically for the task at hand. They must also have the necessary interpersonal skills to interact with a difficult customer who might be upset about a high repair bill or the inconvenience of bringing his or her car in and having to wait while it's fixed. Also, because mechanics often recommend replacing worn parts before they become hazardous or stop functioning completely, customers often become skeptical about paying for parts that aren't broken yet.

On the Job

Auto mechanics work in independently owned repair shops, nationally franchised repair shops, the service departments of new- and used-car dealerships, gas stations, body shops, and for large companies and government agencies whose fleet vehicles require regular maintenance and repair.

The outlook for auto mechanics is bright, because even with fluctuations in the economy, people will still need their services; automobiles aren't luxury items as they were a hundred years ago. This means that qualified mechanics with the right background and training will have no trouble finding employment. According to one study, there is currently a shortage of nearly sixty thousand mechanics, and that number is only expected to grow. Recent trends show that people want to keep their cars longer, which translates to larger numbers of older cars that will need to be properly maintained.

Salaries

Though salaries vary according to the size of the company, location, and how much experience is involved, auto mechanics can expect to receive an average starting salary of $14,000, about $23,000 after five years, and $33,000 after ten years.

Meet and Greet

Dave Friedrich

Dave Friedrich is the auto service manager at Fred's Automotive in Loveland, Colorado. He studied auto mechanics for two years at a community college, and he has attended numerous auto-related classes and seminars through the years.

"No one I know was at all surprised when my first job as a teenager was at a gas station, where I pumped gas, checked oil and tires, washed windows, and did some minor repairs," Friedrich says. "I have been fascinated with cars for as long as I can remember. Once, when I was about six or seven, we spent our vacation at an uncle's farm, and he had an old abandoned pickup truck out back. I spent all day, every day, sitting behind the steering wheel, pretending I was driving. I'd let my little sister sit in the passenger seat and pretend along with me, but I'd never give her a turn behind the wheel! I graduated to 'driving' just a few years later. My dad would sit me on his lap and let me steer the car around a parking lot or back and forth in the driveway. I saved and saved to buy my first car, and then I spent all my spare time working on it, whether it needed anything or not. To this day, I can still remember all the makes, models, and years of all the cars my parents and all my other relatives have owned over the years, and I even have most of the license plates from those cars hanging in my garage.

"I worked in retail for twelve years as the manager of the auto center at a nationwide department store chain and then later as the general manager of an auto parts and service chain store. I got to know some of my regular customers pretty well, and one customer in particular, Fred, kept telling me that he was getting ready to open his own repair shop soon and he wanted me to come work for him. I've been the service manager at his shop for five years now.

"My job is to help diagnose problems, schedule repairs, prepare estimates for customers, and order all the shop's parts. I'm the first and last, and sometimes the only, contact that the customers have with the shop, so I deal with all different kinds of people. We have an excellent reputation with our customers because we're always fair and honest. It really bothers me when someone comes in with a chip on his or her shoulder, certain that all mechanics rip people off and that we're going to do the same. It's my job to explain to them what the problem is, what's the best way to fix it, and how much it will cost, and I can usually get them to calm down and trust our judgment. People tend to get irate when their only modes of transportation are not functioning, so it's very important to treat them with respect and put yourself in their shoes.

"Occasionally, we get someone who just refuses to trust us. For instance, this one woman's car stalled a week after we fixed something on it, and she came in ranting and raving about how we didn't know what we were doing and how she wanted her money back. As it turned out, the only problem was that her gas tank was empty. But those types of people are rare at our shop. We've earned a large base of repeat customers who trust us completely with their cars.

"I almost always remember what kinds of cars people have. Customers especially like it when they come back into the shop after six months or a year and I can still remember the kind of car we worked on and what we did to it. A guy came in recently and started talking about a problem he was having with one of his cars, and I said, 'You must be talking about your Toyota then, not your Ford,' and he was so surprised that I remembered. But it made him feel special, and that's something that's important in earning a customer's trust. You have to treat every car like you would treat your own.

"I especially like diagnosing problems. People call the shop and expect me to diagnose over the phone, and I start to explain how difficult that is, but once they begin describing the problem or imitating the unusual sounds the car is making, I can usually take a guess at what might be wrong with it. You have to know the right questions to ask, though, and then it's kind of like solving a riddle or putting a puzzle together. For instance, a customer calls and tells me the car won't start. So I ask him to tell me exactly what happens when he turns the key. If absolutely nothing happens, it might be that the battery cables are dirty or not connected properly. If he hears a clicking noise, it could be a dead battery. If the engine turns over but the car never starts, it might be a problem with the fuel supply. If the car starts but dies again right away, it could be a carburetor or fuel injection problem. If I ask the right questions, I might even find out that the car doesn't start only on rainy days or very cold days, and that would signal two completely different problems. Of course, the customer has to bring the car in to get the best diagnosis, but it seems as if customers always feel better when they have an idea ahead of time about what the problem might be.

"Since I've always been interested in cars, it was only natural that I would spend my days around them. You have to really like what you do to be happy, so if you love cars and everything about them, auto mechanics is probably a great career for you."

Frank Broderick Jr.

Frank Broderick Jr. is the owner of Broderick's Foreign Car Service in Tucker, Georgia, where he repairs and maintains all types of foreign cars. He attended a technical automotive school for two years and also spent time training with mechanics at an auto dealership.

"I was introduced to automobile repair while in high school, and I took a liking to it," says Broderick. "I always wanted a career that somehow enhanced the lives of people, and helping people to maintain safe, reliable transportation is very rewarding.

"You need a tremendous amount of patience and logical thinking to service cars. You have to be able to diagnose the problem, identify the solution, and then execute the repair. For instance, when a customer brings in a 'dead' car, we conduct a thorough engine analysis. By the time we're done, the car's engine is humming just like it did when it left the factory.

"You must also take a methodical approach to understanding the technology and ingenuity that went into developing the car. It takes years of research, design, and development before a car is actually built in the factory, so a lot of safety and mechanical systems have been woven into the car's design. You must take a comprehensive approach to servicing the car and keeping safety at the core.

"Seeing customers pick up and drive off in cars that had previously given them trouble is very satisfying. It's instant gratification each time a customer picks up his or her car, and it's very rewarding to have satisfied customers.

"My advice is to work hard, study hard, and be fair and honest. Have integrity, and let your conscience be your guide. Remember that behind every dollar you receive is a face. And don't ever take people for granted."

For Additional Information

Automobile Association of America
1415 Kellum Place
Garden City, NJ 11530
www.aaa.com

American Automobile Manufacturers Association
3011 West Grand Boulevard
Detroit, MI 48202

Automotive Service Association, Inc.
P.O. Box 929
Bedford, TX 76021
www.asashop.org

The Alliance of Automobile Manufacturers has offices in Washington, D.C., California, and Michigan:

Alliance of Automobile Manufacturers
Washington Office (Headquarters)
1401 H Street NW, Suite 900
Washington, DC 20005
www.autoalliance.org

California Office
980 Ninth Street, Suite 2200
Sacramento, CA 95814

Southfield, Michigan Office
2000 Town Center, Suite 1140
Southfield, MI 48075

For a directory of accredited trade and technical schools with training programs for mechanics:

Accrediting Commission of Career Schools and Colleges of
    Technology
2101 Wilson Boulevard, Suite 302
Arlington, VA 22201

For a list of automotive mechanic training programs:

National Automotive Technician Education Foundation
13505 Dulles Technology Drive
Herndon, VA 22071
www.natef.org

To contact the organization that administers the certification test:

National Institute for Automotive Service Excellence
13505 Dulles Technology Drive
Herndon, VA 22071
www.asecert.org

CHAPTER SEVEN

Careers in Architecture

In architecture as in all other operative arts, the end must direct the operation. The end is to build well. Well building has three conditions: Commodity, Firmness and Delight. HENRY WATTON

Help Wanted: Architect

Our firm is seeking a degreed, licensed architect with at least five years' experience. Full-time responsibilities include implementation of architectural design and management of our CAD/architectural department.

Candidates must possess interest in hands-on field investigation, repair design, code review, writing specifications, and preparing drawings; have good communication skills; and be willing to travel at least half of the time.

We offer a generous benefit package.

Zeroing In on What an Architect Does

Architects design individual buildings—such as houses and schools—and entire complexes—such as business parks and college campuses. They have to make them look esthetically pleasing, of course, but they also must be sure that they are safe, functional, and economical, and that they meet all of their clients' needs.

Architects meet with their clients to discuss all aspects of the project, including the clients' requirements, budget, and time frame for completion. Before the design phase begins, they sometimes help their clients select a building site and help prepare environmental impact studies. Other predesign services that an architect might offer include conducting feasibility studies and specifying any requirements a design must meet. For instance, an architect may do a study to determine the space requirements needed, based on the number and type of potential users of a building, then prepare drawings and reports for the client to review before the building is designed. Architects may also provide clients with cost analyses, land-use studies, and even long-range land-use planning.

During the design phase, architects develop the plans for the building. These drawings and other written materials must not only show the building's appearance, but also each and every detail of its construction. Drawings of the building's structural systems must be prepared. These include air-conditioning, heating, ventilation, electrical systems, plumbing, and sometimes landscaping. While preparing these plans, architects must strictly adhere to building codes, zoning laws, fire regulations, and special ordinances such as required access for disabled persons. Architects must be prepared for the fact that these plans will probably need to be revised several times during the project, due to the clients' changing needs, budget constraints, and difficulties with contractors.

At the same time that they're revising the plans, architects often help their clients with other aspects of the project, like getting construction bids and selecting contractors. They may also visit the construction site several times during the project to see that the plans are being followed correctly, that the right materials are being used, and that the whole project is staying on schedule. Postconstruction services that architects might offer include facilities management and evaluating how well the finished building is meeting the clients' needs.

There is a good deal of stress associated with being an architect, particularly when there's a deadline to be met. Architects often work long hours on nights and weekends to finish a project. When not working on a specific project, they are actively recruiting new business, even though such self-promotion is difficult for some individuals. Also, much like lawyers and doctors, licensed architects must take all legal responsibility for their work, and this puts a lot of pressure on them.

Qualifications and Training

A vision—a desire to build—a creative imagination—drawing skills. Architects need all these things, but they must also be proficient in engineering, be computer literate, and be good at both oral and written communications. Patience and self-discipline are also important, because the educational road is long, and it's followed by a mandatory three-year internship prior to becoming licensed. Proficiency in computer-aided design and drafting (CADD) is a must. And architects should really love math, too!

There are three different educational options. Most architects choose a five-year bachelor of architecture program, offered by more than one hundred accredited schools. (The only downfall of this course of study is that, because it's very specialized, it's difficult for candidates who change their career plans to make a transition into a nonarchitecture degree program without losing too much ground.) A second option is earning a bachelor of arts degree in a related field, followed by a two-year master of architecture degree. The final option is earning a bachelor's degree in an unrelated field, which must then be followed by a three- or four-year master of architecture degree. The final semester of many programs is usually spent creating an architectural project from start to finish, including preparing a detailed 3-D model.

After graduation, candidates work as intern-architects at firms, training under the close supervision of a licensed architect. Most states require that candidates do this for a period of three years, during which time they assist in preparing drawings, do research on building codes, and generally help in any way the architect needs them to.

During this time, candidates begin studying for the Architect Registration Examination (ARE), which they can take when their three-year internship is completed. Once they pass the ARE and meet any other licensing standards required by the state, they may call themselves architects and may contract to provide architectural services in that state. (Requirements for licensing may vary slightly from state to state.)

Licensed architects are expected to keep up with continual advances in technology by taking classes, attending conferences and seminars, and subscribing to architecture magazines such as *Architectural Digest*.

On the Job

The majority of architects work for small, private design firms, where they might someday advance to a managerial or supervisory role or even become a partner. Though smaller firms may be somewhat limited in the size and scope of projects they work on, architects at these firms can gain valuable, across-the-board experience rather than becoming specialized in one area.

If an architect wants to develop a particular specialty, however, a larger architecture firm affords the perfect opportunity to do so. These firms offer a wider range of project types and sizes, plus the ability to work with very large budgets, and such complex projects must often be tackled by an entire team of specialists.

Other job opportunities for architects exist with government agencies, such as those involved with community planning.

Architects may also work directly for general building contractors. Only a very small number of architects are self-employed.

Licensed architects may also decide to teach at the university level, write books, or lecture. Some end up designing things other than buildings, like furniture or housewares. Some prefer to step in as a consultant when a job is already underway, to advise on such things as what materials to use and ways to keep the project on schedule and within its budget.

Those who earn an architecture degree but decide not to complete the intern-architect requirements or take the licensing exam often seek employment in related fields, such as interior design, graphic design, urban planning, civil engineering, real estate development, or construction management.

One area of architecture that is expected to grow in the near future is the remodeling or complete renovation of older buildings. This will be especially important in dense urban areas where there is no more land to construct new buildings.

Architects who design retail space and office buildings can expect that fluctuations in the economy will affect the need for their services. However, those who design institutional buildings, such as schools, hospitals, and churches, will be less affected by the economy.

Salaries

Salaries for architects can vary considerably depending on the area of the country, the experience of the professional, the employer, and the nature of the project. Median compensation for architects is about $50,000. Experienced architects can earn between $70,000 and $100,000, and firm principals and partners can earn $130,000 or more.

Meet and Greet

Andrea B. Dibner

Andrea Dibner is a senior associate at Tobin + Parnes Design Enterprises in New York. She received a bachelor of architecture degree from the Pratt Institute in Brooklyn, and a master of engineering degree from the Steven's Institute in New Jersey. She has received several awards and commendations for her work, including awards for outstanding achievement in the profession and for excellence in total design, from the New York Society of Architects.

"After eighteen years of schooling, I began working for a Pratt professor who owned a design/build architecture and engineering firm," explains Dibner. "I worked at this firm for approximately four years, doing structural engineering, construction management, and design/build projects while attending graduate school at night for my master's. During this time, I established a working relationship with the firm that I am currently working with now. When I decided to leave the realm of engineering and come back to architecture, I left to work for a small architectural firm for approximately four months, until I received a phone call from Robert Parnes, my current boss, asking me if I was interested in working for him and his partner. Tobin + Parnes was able to offer me the types of projects and growth potential that I was looking for. For the past three years, with the help, trust, and guidance of my bosses and peers, I have been able to strengthen my architectural and construction management skills. I suppose that my constant drive to always learn and try new things has brought me to where I am today—not to mention a little bit of wanting to prove to others that I could do it better than it had been done before.

"As a senior associate, I am responsible for designing, detailing, and managing all types and sizes of architectural projects from start to finish. One of the current projects that I am working on is the reconstruction of the marquee and arch at the Paramount Building in New York City. This project involves the use of current technology (for example, fiber optic lighting systems, glass-fiber reinforced concrete, fiber reinforced plastic, LED) to replicate the intricate and costly architectural details of 1920s ornate architecture. It involves tight schedules and budgets, as well as the replication of original sculpture from historic photographs and research. No useful drawings of the original marquee and arch could be located, so artists and sculptors have had to re-create the original sculpture from historic photographs and studies of the architecture from the 1920s. It has proven to be one of the most challenging projects that I have worked on to date. I am constantly looking ahead to predict what may lie around the corner and finding new ways to solve old problems. Through this struggle, I have learned to appreciate the value of past architecture and the time, pride, dedication, and love that the original architects and artisans had for their work.

"When I was a child, my parents exposed me to the design/ build environment and also to the high-fashion manufacturing industry. At the age of five, I was sewing my own clothes, as well as some for my dogs! I also had a very keen ability for taking apart and putting things back together again. Furthermore, I enjoyed working with my hands and was told that I had a good design sense. Originally, I thought I would become a graphic designer because I enjoyed the process and fast pace of the profession, but I found that I was happier being knee-deep in tools and dirt. By choosing architecture, I was able to combine my mathematical, logical side with my sensitive, hands-on, and adventurous side. I find that, through architecture, I have the ability to work at larger-than-life scales down to the most minute details, such as picking the type of screw that will fasten down a piece of wood. Architecture can be endless or simply defined at any moment— a metaphor that I feel defines my life at times.

"The biggest surprise that I have encountered on my journey is the lack of awareness regarding the amount of work that goes into an architectural project. People sometimes do not realize that the artist's idea/concept is what brings life to the project, design, or space. But I suppose that making it look easy and effortless is the mark of a project's success.

"Architects have to continually think forward and backward during a project and understand how each piece of the project relates to and affects the other elements involved. They must constantly think in three dimensions, understanding how the plan, section, and elevation come together to create a building. If one element of a project is changed, the architect methodically reviews the change and will identify and systematically solve the changes that will be encountered throughout the remainder of the project.

"Seeing the work that I have designed and labored tirelessly over gives me a sense of pride and accomplishment. From the smallest detail to an entire building or complex, it is great to see a mark on paper turn into reality.

"The best advice anyone ever gave me is that you must love what you do. You must be willing to breathe, think, and sleep architecture continually, and to make the sacrifices that are required of you as an artist and design professional. With the time and effort it takes to complete a project, I have found that my personal life and dreams, which are never outside the realm of architecture and design, sometimes must take a backseat to my profession.

"Architecture is a profession for the dedicated and consistently driven individual. For me, one of the rewards is self-satisfaction—although projects can be complicated by various unforeseen obstacles. With the advancements in technology, building materials, and global affairs, the architect is constantly learning and trying to develop new and stimulating environments. Despite the challenges, I find myself excited every time I find a building or object that possesses greatness in design and engineering. The fact that a person or persons has created this object makes me want to try harder and work more, so that one day someone will come and look at my work and say 'this was done by a person who understood architecture/design to its fullest.'"

Robert Mark Parnes

Robert Mark Parnes is an architect and one of the principals of Tobin + Parnes Design Enterprises in New York City. He received a bachelor of architecture in 1969 from the Pratt Institute in Brooklyn, New York, and earned his New York State Architects License in 1973. He also earned licenses in two other states, New Jersey (1980) and Illinois (1998).

"I have gotten to where I am today by working very, very, very hard every single day since 1964, when I entered the Pratt Institute to study architecture," says Parnes. "I am currently one of the two principals of Tobin + Parnes Design Enterprises, a full-service architectural and interior design firm, which was founded in December of 1983. We have a variety of projects that we are working on right now, such as the redesign of various facilities at the Hebrew Home for the Aged in Riverdale, Bronx, New York; a Japanese restaurant in Times Square; a ten thousand-square-foot adult technical school; the expansion of an Italian restaurant in Times Square, a yoga studio; and the project we are most proud of, the restoration of the former Paramount Theater marquee and surrounding arch in the heart of Times Square. We have worked on the restoration of many of the historic elements of this building, which is a New York City Landmarks Preservation Commission–designated landmark. Included in the restoration projects are the globe at the top of the building, four clock faces on the tower, and the lighting at the building setbacks.

"When I was about five years old, my father, a tool- and die maker, took courses at night school to learn how to read and draw technical drawings for the molds that he made and serviced. I would play with his school toys—a T-square, triangle, and drawing board (which I still have)—that he used to draw details for his class. The tools were fun to use, and I asked him who used them. He told me that a draftsman would use the tools to make drawings, so I told him that I wanted to be a draftsman. He looked at me and said, 'Don't be a draftsman. Be the best. Be an architect.' That is all I ever knew I wanted to be. In the lower grades, I had displayed some artistic ability above the average for my age group, and in high school I excelled in mechanical drawing. I was not a great student but managed to get into Pratt.

"I don't think there has been a biggest surprise or largest challenge. I think my whole life has been a surprise on some level, and my life has been the biggest challenge. I was surprised at the amount of work and dedication that was required of me to keep up with the work at Pratt. Staying the course was an enormous challenge. I worked hard for five years, including working while going to school, and I managed to graduate with a degree in architecture. Of the 175 students who started as freshmen, 44 graduated, and half were transfers from other schools and programs. It was a surprise when I entered the real world and had to forget some of what I learned in school in order to survive. It was a surprise to be treated just like anyone else; after all, I was an architect.

"It was a challenge to work with other architects and feel that I had something to contribute. It was a surprise that this kid from the Bronx was able to move ahead in the architectural field and be heard. It was a challenge, as afraid as I was, to start my own business with a great friend, at a time when my first child was weeks old and I had left a job after ten years. It was a surprise that the business started to succeed and that it has lasted this long. It was a challenge and surprise to survive the recession of the late 1980s, and the challenge will continue in these times. I would love to be surprised once more!

"Puzzle solving and methodical thinking are what this career is all about. Architects are somewhat like orchestra conductors: they know how the instruments are supposed to sound, but they may not be able to play all of them. Our instruments are the other professionals we work with—various structural, mechanical, and electrical engineers; lighting experts; sound and video consultants; and other contractors who have expertise in a variety of fields. We know the parts each professional or consultant plays in the scope of the project, although we may not have the same knowledge they do.

"Our projects are all puzzles; however, at the beginning of a project, we don't know how many pieces there are or what the size of the pieces will be until we understand the complexity of the issues needing to be solved. Buildings and spaces are designed to solve use issues for our clients, and we must understand how the project will ultimately be used. Some projects have a long list of requirements that must be solved by the building or space. We must methodically think through how the final facility must work for the people who use it, and this becomes the puzzle to be solved. Adding pieces to the puzzle are the various building and other codes that govern many aspects of the design process. The codes require certain dimensions for stairs, corridors, doors, windows, wheelchair access, distances between exit doors, and so on. The codes also dictate fire ratings of materials and combinations of materials, and they require concentration and methodical understanding in order to apply them to the puzzle of design.

"When we work through all of the space usage issues and solve the puzzle, we then must decide how to build the project. What materials will be used, and what materials are best suited for each segment of the project? You would not use carpet in a restaurant kitchen, for instance. Do we use structural steel for a building or poured concrete or wood? Do we use wood doors or metal or glass? Do we need elevators and escalators or are stairs sufficient? How big do the toilets have to be? Putting any project together is solving a great puzzle. Each project becomes a new puzzle, and the solving of the puzzle is in the methodical approach to the answers.

"There is no part of this job that I would consider the best. Everything about being an architect and practicing architecture is the best. Starting out with a blank piece of paper and ultimately having a tangible space or building at the end of the process is very fulfilling and satisfying. Working with clients and understanding their needs and desires, thinking through the various aspects of each project, and then providing the information that will allow the space or building to be built is the best. Having the client say that they got what they wanted and confirming that we listened well is the best.

"I also can't say that there is one person who stands out as giving me the best advice. There have been many people over the years that have given me good advice that has led to my being where I am today.

"Do not become an architect if you think it will lead to untold monetary riches. Do become an architect if you have a passion for the design process, experience a thrill every time you walk into a building or space that makes you feel exhilarated, are committed to hard work and long hours, and feel rewarded by seeing your mind's vision become a reality in brick and mortar. Architecture is not 9 A.M. to 5 P.M., five days a week. Architecture is a way of life.

"There are so many aspects to serving as an architect that it is hard to cover all of them. Some architects are content with focusing on only one aspect of the profession; for example, some architects just want to design. Others are satisfied with doing construction documents; some like to write specifications. Then there are those of us who like to try and do it all. It makes for a very challenging, exciting, and overall satisfying way of life."

For Additional Information

American Architectural Foundation
1735 New York Avenue NW
Washington, DC 20006
www.archfoundation.org

American Institute of Architects
1735 New York Avenue NW
Washington, DC 20006
www.aiaonline.com

National Architectural Accrediting Board
1735 New York Avenue NW
Washington, DC 20006
www.naab.org

CHAPTER EIGHT

Careers in Private Detecting and Investigating

Discovery consists of looking at the same thing as everyone else and thinking something different. ALBERT SZENT-GYORGYI

Help Wanted: Private Investigator

We are seeking a full-time licensed private investigator to add to our staff. Full benefits offered to experienced, serious professionals. Must be willing to travel with little notice.
Please respond immediately.

Zeroing In on What a Private Detective or Investigator Does

Is there a little bit of Sherlock Holmes in you? If so, read on. Private detectives and investigators assist attorneys, government agencies, businesses, and the public with a variety of problems, such as gathering facts, tracing debtors, finding relatives or friends who have lost touch, or conducting background investigations. The primary job of private investigators and some private detectives is to obtain information and locate assets or individuals. Some private detectives protect stores and hotels from theft, vandalism, and disorder.

Private detectives working as general investigators have duties ranging from locating missing persons to exposing fraudulent workers' compensation claims. Some investigators specialize in one field, such as finance, where they might use accounting skills to investigate the financial standing of a company or locate funds stolen by an embezzler.

About half of all private investigators are self-employed or work for detective agencies. They specialize in missing persons, infidelity, and background investigations, including financial profiles and asset searches; physical surveillance; on-line computer database searches; and insurance investigations. They may obtain information, interview witnesses, and assemble evidence for litigation or criminal trials.

Many investigators spend considerable time conducting surveillance in the hope that they will observe inconsistencies in a subject's behavior. For example, a person who has recently filed a workers' compensation claim that an injury has made walking difficult should not be able to jog or mow the lawn. If such behavior is observed, the investigator takes video or still photographs to document the activity and reports back to the supervisor or client.

Stakeouts are a common form of surveillance. On a stakeout, an investigator regularly observes a site, such as the home of a subject, until the desired evidence is obtained. Armed with cameras (both still and video), binoculars, and a citizen's band radio or a cell phone, the investigator situates himself or herself in an inconspicuous location waiting for information to emerge.

Some investigations involve verification of facts, such as an individual's place of employment or income. Thus, a phone call or visit to the workplace might be necessary. In other investigations, especially in missing persons cases, the investigator interviews people to learn as much as possible about an individual's previous movements. These interviews can be formal or informal and sometimes turn into confrontations if the person is uncooperative.

Legal investigators specialize in cases involving the courts and lawyers. To assist in preparing criminal defenses, investigators locate witnesses, interview police, gather and review evidence, take photographs, and testify in court. To assist attorneys in the preparation of litigation for injured parties, they interview prospective witnesses, collect information on the parties involved in litigation, and search out testimonial, documentary, or physical evidence.

Corporate investigators work for companies that are not investigative firms—often large corporations. In contrast to most private investigators, they report to a corporate chain of command wherein they conduct internal or external investigations. External investigations focus on preventing criminal schemes, thefts of company assets, and fraudulent deliveries of products by suppliers. In internal investigations, they ensure that expense accounts are not abused and catch employees who are stealing.

Investigators who specialize in finance may be hired to investigate the financial standing of companies or individuals. These investigators often work with investment bankers and lawyers. They generally develop confidential financial profiles of individuals or companies who may be parties to large financial transactions. An asset search is a common type of such an investigation.

Private detectives and investigators who work for large retail stores or shopping malls are responsible for loss control and asset protection. Store detectives safeguard the assets of retail stores by apprehending persons attempting to steal merchandise or destroy store property. They detect theft by shoplifters, vendor representatives, delivery personnel, and even store employees. Store detectives also conduct periodic inspections of stock areas, dressing rooms, and rest rooms, and sometimes they assist in the opening and closing of the store. They may be required to prepare loss prevention and security reports for management and testify in court against persons they apprehend.

Computers have changed the nature of this profession and have become an integral part of investigative work. They allow investigators to obtain massive amounts of information in a short period of time from the dozens of on-line databases containing probate records, motor-vehicle registrations, credit reports, association membership lists, and other information.

Based on the need to conduct surveillance and contact people who may not be available during normal working hours, private investigators often work irregular hours, including mornings, evenings, weekends, and holidays. Investigators who work solely for insurance companies and corporate investigators have more normal work hours.

Many investigators spend much time away from their offices conducting interviews or doing surveillance, but some work in an office most of the day conducting computer searches and making phone calls. Corporate investigators often split their time between the office and the field; work done in the office generally consists of computer research.

When away from the office, the environment might range from plush boardrooms to seedy bars. Store and hotel detectives work mostly in the businesses that they protect. Investigators generally work alone but sometimes work with others during surveillance or stakeouts.

Much of the work that detectives and investigators do can be confrontational because the person being observed may not wish to be observed. Thus, the job can be quite stressful and sometimes dangerous. As a result, some investigators carry handguns.

Qualifications and Training

There are no formal education requirements for most private detective and investigator jobs, although most employers prefer high school graduates. In fact, many private detectives have college degrees.

Some private detectives and investigators get their entry-level training on the job while working for insurance or collections companies or in the security industry. Many investigators enter from the military or law enforcement jobs and apply their experience as law enforcement officers, military police, or government agents. Other investigators enter from such diverse fields as finance, accounting, investigative reporting, insurance, and law. These individuals often can apply their prior work experience in a related investigation specialty.

The vast majority of states and the District of Columbia require that private investigators be licensed. Licensing requirements vary widely among the states, but in most the state police department is the licensing authority. Some states have very liberal requirements, while others have stringent regulations. For example, the California Department of Consumer Affairs Bureau of Security and Investigative Services requires six thousand hours of investigative experience, a background check, a qualifying score on a written examination, payment of a $50 application fee and a $32 fingerprint fee, plus payment of an annual $175 license fee upon approval. In contrast, other states may have few or no licensing requirements.

A growing number of states are enacting mandatory training programs for private investigators. In states that require licensing, a felony conviction generally disqualifies a candidate from being granted a license.

In most investigation firms, the screening process for potential employees includes a background check consisting of confirmation of education, work experience and criminal history, and interviews with references and others known to the applicant. Corporate and industrial security positions may require a criminal history check, a personal interview, an ethics interview, a practical test, verification of education claims, and license review, as well as personal and employment reference checks.

For private detective and investigator jobs, most employers look for individuals with ingenuity who are aggressive, persistent, and assertive. A candidate must not be afraid of being confrontational, should communicate well, and should be able to think on his or her feet. The courts are often the ultimate judge of a properly conducted investigation, so the investigator must be able to present the facts in a manner a jury will believe.

Training in subjects such as criminal justice is helpful to the aspiring private detective. Most corporate investigators must have a bachelor's degree, preferably in a business-related field. Some corporate investigators have master's degrees in business administration or law degrees, while others are certified.

Corporate investigators hired by larger companies may receive formal training from their employers on business practices, management structure, and various finance-related topics. Interview and interrogation training is frequently included.

Most investigation firms are small, with little room for advancement. Usually there are no defined ranks or steps, so advancement is in terms of salary and assignment status. Many investigators work for an investigation firm in the beginning of their investigative careers and after a few years try to start their own investigation firms. Corporate and legal investigators may rise to supervisor or manager of the security or investigation department.

Salaries

Earnings of private detectives and investigators vary greatly depending on the employer, specialty, and geographical area in which they work. According to a recent study by Abbott, Langer & Associates, private investigators average about $36,700 a year, and store detectives about $16,100.

According to other limited information, legal investigators earn an estimated $15,000 to $18,000 a year to start, and experienced legal investigators earn $20,000 to $35,000. Entry-level corporate investigators earn an estimated $40,000 to $45,000 annually, and experienced corporate investigators earn $50,000 to $55,000. Most private investigators bill their clients between $50 and $150 per hour. However, private investigators, except for those working for large corporations, do not receive paid vacation or sick days, health or life insurance, retirement packages, or other benefits. Investigators are usually reimbursed for expenses and given a car allowance.

In contrast, most corporate investigators receive health insurance, pension plans, profit-sharing plans, and paid vacation.

Meet and Greet

Susan Giller

Susan Giller is a private investigator in Bethesda, Maryland, where she heads her own investigation firm, Susan Giller & Associates.

"I have a law degree and a master's degree in social work," Giller says. "I worked as an investigative reporter for five years prior to becoming a private investigator and also worked as a staff investigator for a law firm before opening my own business in 1981. I provide investigative services for law firms, companies, the media, government agencies, and private individuals.

"I knew this was the field for me because it is very much in sync with my personality. Most of my cases are puzzles I have to solve, and I like helping people with problems. I like the variety, challenge, and fun of this job. I also like being my own boss and setting my own hours.

"Being a good investigator is not really something that can be taught. You either think like an investigator, or you don't. You either have the type of personality to get people to help you, or you don't. You're either a resourceful person, or you're not. You're either persistent and refuse to take no for an answer, or you give up when faced with obstacles. You either have the right personality traits for this work, or you don't.

"So before you pursue this career, answer these questions: Do you have courage? Are you naturally curious? Do you like solving problems? Can you challenge people who are in positions of authority? Are you able to engage people of all types and get them to trust you and want to help you? Are you a good writer? Are you thorough? Are you clever and resourceful? Do you think outside the box?

"If you want to be a private investigator, become a reporter first. It's a job that requires similar skills. If you can't be a reporter, you probably won't be a good investigator. But if you're a really good reporter, you'll probably do well in investigation.

"The best advice anyone ever gave me? Don't take no for an answer!"

Nate T. Lenow Jr.

Nate T. Lenow Jr. is the president of Lenow International, Inc., a private investigation firm based in Memphis, Tennessee. Lenow earned a B.A. in sociology and an M.A. in criminal justice, both from the University of Memphis. His professional certifications include Certified Protection Professional from the American Society for Industrial Security and Certified Fraud Examiner from the Association of Certified Fraud Examiners. He has attended numerous educational seminars on the topics of investigation and security, and his specialties are fraud investigation, computer forensics, and forensic security.

"I didn't really pursue this field at first; I was assigned to do investigative work in my job as a social service caseworker," explains Lenow. "However, looking back on it, I was always curious and loved to discover things. When I was about five years old, I took on my first 'case' and tracked down a pal who took my toy fire truck. Then, when I was around twelve, I was 'framed' for carving some words into the piano bench at my piano instructor's studio. By getting all of my fellow piano students to write out some words on paper, I was able to identify the girl who actually did it because she misspelled a word on the paper the same way it was misspelled on the piano bench.

"There have been many surprises and challenges for me. The one that seems most notable is proving the innocence of a man accused of a serious crime. In fact, his innocence was proven to the extent that charges were dropped without a trial. The investigation took about six months, and there was no money to fund the investigation. At first, everything was stacked up against me, but I was able to turn it all around. During the entire course of the investigation, there was considerable pressure on me to find the proof of his innocence because he was in jail the entire time. He was also a friend of mine, which of course added to the pressure.

"Each investigation presents you with a situation that you must resolve to a successful conclusion. You must think logically to understand or determine what happened. You must be methodical in your thinking to prevent any personal bias or outside influence that might keep you from successfully resolving the matter. I am always looking for new ways to improve my logical thinking; I find that flowcharts are very useful in identifying connections between various facts or events. I also like to review a case on its conclusion, to see what errors I might have made in logic or methodology.

"The best way to become an investigator is to pursue an investigative job in government service. You will accumulate a lot of experience and receive good training. I especially like the independence and variety of the job. Any job has its dull spots, and this is no exception. But most times, it can be quite exciting.

"Early in my investigative career, when I worked in government, I was assigned by my agency to work with Special Agent Horace Ramsey of the United States Department of Agriculture, to investigate a major food stamp fraud. Every day that I worked with him, he would find a way to weave the words 'don't assume anything' into the conversation. So, my advice is: don't assume anything. This is truly the investigator's creed."

Robert A. Gardner

Robert Gardner is a security and crime risk advisor in Ventura, California, and Las Vegas, Nevada. He holds private investigator licenses in both states and also holds many other licenses, certifications, and credentials, including California Private Patrol Operator, Certified Protection Professional, Certified Security Professional, Police Firearms Instructor, and Advanced and Supervisory Peace Officer.

Gardner earned an associate in science degree in administration of justice/law enforcement and is a graduate of the Department of Defense Information School and the U.S. Army Infantry Officer Candidate School. In addition, he has more than three thousand hours of advanced training in security/loss prevention management, law enforcement, emergency management, media relations, and other areas, and he holds memberships in ten professional associations. In Gardner's current position, he provides to business such services as security adequacy evaluation, crime risk assessment, workplace violence prevention, emergency planning, and physical security design.

"Actually, I don't think I chose this career; it chose me," Gardner says. "I started out to be a journalist, but very early on, I realized that watching the action from the distance and just writing about it didn't provide the level of excitement I wanted. My first attempt at finding real excitement led to a three-year tour as an army infantry officer during the Vietnam War. While it was certainly exciting, a job that involved jumping out of moving helicopters into bullet-riddled rice paddies was not my dream career.

"After my time in the army, I more or less stumbled into the world of security and retail loss prevention. Thanks to my military background, I found work as a retail security manager. The work was interesting, and my journalism training came in handy for writing investigation reports, but the position still didn't offer the level of excitement I was looking for. Since there is considerable interaction between retail security and law enforcement, I got to know several police officers, and I realized that their jobs seemed more exciting than mine. That prompted me to become a police officer. No more standing outside the yellow police tape as a journalist or catching shoplifters as a retail security agent; now I was inside the tape, where the real excitement was.

"Not long after I became a cop, crime prevention came into its own as a recognized law enforcement tool. Thanks to my background in security and loss prevention, I was transferred to my department's new crime prevention unit. Much to my surprise, I found that preventing crime was much more exciting than fighting it.

"The surprises and challenges of this career actually go hand in hand; both have to do with how people view security and crime prevention. My biggest surprise continues to be how little real interest most business managers and public officials have in addressing security and crime prevention issues. In spite of the civil liability ramifications and fiscal impacts of crime, relatively few political and business leaders actively assess the security and crime risks and institute meaningful policies and procedures to protect their communities and the business facilities in them.

"I just formed the CERAHS Project, a Nevada-based non-profit organization dedicated to public safety advocacy. The project will provide a variety of services to assist community groups, concerned individuals, and public agencies in assuring that a concern for public safety is a central element in the community planning and development process.

"*Crime prevention* is defined as the anticipation, the recognition, and the appraisal of crime risks and the initiation of actions to remove or reduce those risks. It can also be defined as a pattern of attitudes and behaviors directed both at reducing the threat of crime and enhancing the sense of safety and security and at positively influencing the quality of life in our society to help develop environments where crime cannot flourish. Under each definition, there is a requirement to arrive at a means of deterring crime. In order to reach that point, it is necessary to solve the puzzle of what combinations of circumstances and conditions encourage or discourage criminal activity. Successful security consultants are good at working through this process.

"Far too many people are paralyzed by a fear of making mistakes or being criticized for their decisions. The ability to make decisions and take positions on issues sets the few leaders apart from the many followers. If you are willing to take charge and make decisions, even at the risk of occasionally being wrong, you are likely to find that, more often than not, you will be remembered as the person to look to for answers. This is an enviable position for a security consultant.

"Maintain your independence and integrity. Tell people what they need to know, not what they want to hear."

For Additional Information

Most states have associations for private detectives and investigators that provide career information. For information on local licensing requirements, contact your local state police headquarters.

National Association of Investigative Specialists
P.O. Box 33244
Austin, TX 78764
www.pinais.com

National Association of Legal Investigators
6109 Meadowwood
Grand Blanc, MI 48439
www.nali.com

CHAPTER NINE

Careers in Investigative Reporting

Reporters thrive on the world's misfortune. For this reason they often take an indecent pleasure in events that dismay the rest of humanity.
RUSSELL BAKER

Help Wanted: Investigative Reporter

The *Shoreland Valley Daily Bulletin*, which has a daily circulation of seventy thousand and covers fifteen cities in the suburban Chicago area, is seeking an experienced, skilled reporter to cover an ongoing joint federal-local investigation into corruption. Strong writing and investigative skills are a must. The candidate must be knowledgeable in state and federal public records law and familiar with governmental infrastructure.

Send resume and clips to Meredith Security, Managing Editor.

Zeroing In on What an Investigative Reporter Does

Investigative reporters are the watchdogs of society, the journalistic sleuths who want to protect the public from unethical government officials, dishonest companies, unsafe products, environmental pollutants, and money-making schemes. They're activists and reformers who stay firmly planted on the side of truth and fairness, pursuing and exposing corruption. Concerned only with the common good, they independently monitor those in power.

On the Job

Though all reporters are involved with reporting the news, investigative reporters differ from general assignment reporters and beat reporters in many important ways. General assignment reporters must rush to the scene of a breaking news story, gather information quickly, conduct short interviews, and then report exactly what happened through a hastily prepared broadcast segment or news story. Beat reporters are assigned to a specific subject area, such as education or crime, and they both cover breaking news and write occasional in-depth stories within that subject area.

Investigative reporters, on the other hand, follow up on the original, breaking stories to see if there are unanswered questions that must be investigated for the good of the public. They often spend days, weeks, even months or years on the same story, until they are certain that they have contacted all the available sources, examined all the pertinent documents, and checked and double-checked all the facts.

In fact, general assignment or beat reporters and investigative reporters can be compared to police officers and police detectives, respectively, because one prepares the initial report about what happened and the other investigates further to uncover why it happened (and, in many cases, if it could happen again).

Almost all news stories written by general assignment reporters have the potential of leading to investigative reports. Watergate began as routine coverage of a burglary and eventually led to the resignation of the president. The report of a tragic railroad accident might lead to the discovery that the conductor fell asleep on the job, which in turn could lead to allegations that the railroad is guilty of overworking its employees. Likewise, further investigation of declining test scores at the local high school could uncover the fact that more students than ever before are skipping classes, which might in turn lead to a story about teens hanging out at a local bar that's guilty of serving minors.

Unless they hold a very specialized niche at a large daily newspaper or television station, investigative reporters should be prepared to cover a wide variety of topics, from law enforcement, government corruption, and business scams to stories about the environment or health care. Not every scandal can be exposed; investigative reporters must realize that, during the course of their careers, they will cover both high-impact stories and those that don't end up having much of an impact at all. The high-impact stories, however, often have the potential of changing the participants' lives in negative ways, and investigative reporters must be prepared to live with the results of their exposés, even if it means that their subjects might, for example, lose their jobs or go to prison.

When it comes to the irregular working hours and strict deadlines, investigative journalists feel the same stress that other reporters do, but they have additional pressures to deal with as well. They are not always given the time and budget they need to conduct a thorough investigation, but they still cannot cut any corners, since getting the wrong information and possibly pointing blame at the wrong people could lead to libel lawsuits for the publication (and/or grave damage to the reporter's professional respect and credibility). Since investigative reporters have no more of a right to certain information than average citizens, they must abide by laws and limitations; they, of course, cannot break the law in their pursuit of information (no trespassing on private property, for instance), no matter how vital the desired information might be in proving the allegations.

They are also forced to restrain from letting any personal bias or strong feelings about a subject cloud their judgment and, therefore, detract from the investigation.

Investigative reporters must also tread very lightly when it comes to cultivating relationships with their contacts (also called sources, informants, and whistle-blowers). Many of these people may be extremely reluctant to get involved and talk to the press because their jobs (and, in extreme cases, their lives) might be in danger. This means the investigative reporters must know how to convince their contacts that they can be trusted and will not reveal the contacts' identities.

Reporters who want to break the high-profile stories and make a difference in the community, state, country, or even the world find that investigative journalism is the best way to accomplish their goals.

Qualifications and Training

Investigative reporting is especially suited to journalists who truly believe in the watchdog role of the press (watching over the powerful few on behalf of the many). They must have a passion for uncovering wrongdoings and injustices, and they must often rely on their instincts and experiences to help them decide exactly what is wrong and what is unjust and whether it's important that the public knows the truth about a particular matter. Investigative journalists must be skeptical, persistent (especially when dealing with unresponsive sources), patient (to endure long, involved investigations), aggressive, self-motivated, and creative (with their writing, but also with finding new ways to get information). Most investigative journalists are experienced general assignment or beat reporters who have already paid their dues for several years at a newspaper or television station. During this time, they have probably built up a network of trustworthy sources, learned who's who at various government agencies and companies, discovered how to access and interpret important documents, and honed their interviewing skills.

The educational qualifications for investigative reporters are the same as for other journalists—a college degree is almost always required. Some newspapers and television stations prefer that candidates have a journalism degree, but many believe that a broad liberal arts background is preferable. For those candidates who know they definitely want to specialize in a certain area, such as foreign affairs or state government, a double major or master's degree is helpful. Preparation can also begin in high school, with a well-rounded, college preparatory course of study that includes a concentration in grammar, literature, and creative writing.

While in college, candidates should pursue internships that provide valuable on-the-job experience, even if the pay is low or nonexistent. Internships not only look impressive on a resume, they often lead to employment at that very newspaper or television station. On-campus newspapers and radio stations often have positions available as well.

Investigative reporters are found almost everywhere other journalists are found—at daily and weekly newspapers, radio stations, television stations, and magazines. Larger publications and stations often have several investigative reporters, each covering a different area, such as the state government, education, or consumer alerts.

Fortunately, investigative reporting knows no geographical boundaries; there are jobs nearly everywhere. An investigative reporter working for a weekly newspaper in a tiny Midwestern farm town needs the same journalistic skills and personality traits and uses the same investigative tools and procedures as an investigative reporter who works for a national news bureau headquartered in Washington, D.C. And, while the potential for uncovering a high-profile story is probably greater in a large city than it is in a rural area, a story with far-reaching consequences, such as one exposing the detrimental health effects of a certain industry, for instance, will have the same impact on society no matter where it originated.

Most entry-level reporting jobs are with small publications, so small-town and suburban newspapers offer the most opportunities for beginners. Local radio, TV, and cable stations (particularly in larger cities) also offer opportunities for reporters.

Overall employment for journalists is expected to grow very little, due to mergers, consolidations, and closures of newspapers and decreased circulation, but some growth is expected in online newspapers and magazines and other new media areas.

Salaries

According to the United States Department of Labor, salaries for investigative reporters vary widely. However, median annual earnings are about $25,000. The middle 50 percent earn between $18,000 and $38,000, and the lowest 10 percent earn less than $13,000. The highest ten percent earn more than $70,000. Those with considerable experience can earn $75,000 to $100,000.

Salary figures are apt to be considerably higher in New York and California. Also, the larger the employer, the greater the opportunity for a higher salary.

Meet and Greet

Marisol Bello

Marisol Bello works as an investigative reporter at the *Pittsburgh Tribune-Review*.

"I graduated with a B.A. in journalism and Latin American studies from New York University," says Bello. "During college, I interned anywhere that would give me the time of day, starting with a small local weekly in the Bronx. I rewrote press releases and edited and laid out the paper with the only other staffer, the paper's editor. I worked my way to an internship with *New York Newsday*, the paper that gave me the first taste of working for a big city tabloid, a skill that would come in handy later in my career. At *Newsday*, I covered fires, murders, and news features. My first 'real' job was as a feature writer with the *Dayton Daily News*, where I covered fashion and trend stories about young people. I didn't have any experience doing it, but I muddled through it and enjoyed it a lot.

"Later, I moved to the *Philadelphia Daily News*, a gritty newspaper that thrived on murders and scandals for its front page. I covered education, courts, and the crime beat. I wrote stories about cop killings, mothers killing newborn babies, and husbands killing wives. One of the biggest stories I covered was the trial of a bat-wielding gang of suburban thugs who bludgeoned a teenager to death. The gang beat the boy on the steps of the Catholic church where he had been an altar boy. The story sparked a furor with the 9-1-1 system because operators were rude and dismissed the neighbors who were calling to report the beating. The other big story was the murder of the secretary of Delaware's governor by a prominent married attorney with whom she was having an affair. The attorney dumped her body in the ocean in a fishing cooler. The cooler later washed up on a New Jersey beach and helped convict the attorney. He is facing the death penalty.

"Currently, I'm a projects reporter at the *Tribune-Review*. I work on investigative stories, such as a three-month project that looked at why the city of Pittsburgh was in a deep financial crisis. I went on the campaign trail for the 2000 election, and I traveled to Haiti for another special project. I also generate stories—working with databases that help you find everything,

from the most unsafe bridges in the country to the most dangerous colleges and the crimes that occur on their campuses.

"I've been in love with journalism since the tenth grade, when
I took a journalism class and worked for my school's paper. I
couldn't get over seeing my name in print and watching other
people read my stories. There is definitely some vanity in why I
love this job.

"The challenges over the years change as you move along the
career path. At first, the biggest challenge for me was talking to
people, interviewing them, and getting them to share secrets.
Over the years, as I've developed, that's become easier because
I've learned to treat my sources as individuals and really listen
and be interested in what they have to say.

"The fact that I am a newspaper writer presents the challenge
for me. Writing a story to a specific length, making it interesting,
and trying to make it better all the time is an ongoing battle, one
I don't think I'll ever conquer. But that's a good thing.

"Puzzle solving and methodical thinking are key to becoming
a successful journalist. In this business, you're always running
into people, bureaucracies, organizations, and companies that
don't want you to get the information you are seeking. To really
achieve in this career, you have to find ways around that. You
have to find out where else you can get the information you need
when doors are shutting all around you.

"The most incredible part of the job is that it can be the most
exciting thing in the world. How else can you meet the president
and regularly brush elbows with the mayor, the governor, celebri-
ties, and all the people making an impact in your community?

"There's also no more amazing feeling than when you're working on a big breaking story (a political scandal, close elections,
and so forth) and you're trying to get all the information as
quickly as possible. The adrenaline that rushes through you is
unparalleled. Working on any story that you love, whether it is a
breaking story, a court trial, or an investigative piece, is what
makes this worth doing. There is a tremendous satisfaction when

you finish writing the story, you know you did a good job, and you see it run on the front page the next day.

"Then there's the connection you make with people when you're working on certain kinds of stories. During my career, I've met a lot of people who have lost loved ones in tragic ways. I've met homeless people and junkies and the downtrodden. And one of the special things about my job is being able to tell their stories, not by making them seem pathetic or by being condescending, but by listening to them, showing compassion, and relating their experiences honestly.

"My mother once told me, 'You don't know how to do everything, so relax and don't beat yourself up if you don't do it right the first time.' At eighteen or nineteen, I was brought to tears at a candlelight vigil in the Bronx for an eight-year-old girl who had disappeared while playing near her house. It was my first time covering a live news story; television cameras, photographers, and reporters from New York City's major media were all there. I was intimidated and didn't know how to interview people and get them to talk. I bumbled through and managed to get enough quotes for a story for the local weekly where I worked part-time, but I was so disappointed in myself because I hadn't risen to the occasion. But my mom had been right, of course. This is a tough job, and you never stop learning the craft and learning about yourself. But it becomes easier the more you make yourself open to learning and listening.

"To be successful, you really have to love this field. You have to love the stories and the intrigue and the people. You have to commit to it because it's not a nine-to-five desk job. You work long hours, you don't always get treated well by the people you're attempting to interview, you have to deal with a lot of mundane nonsense, and you'll never get rich doing it. The satisfaction truly comes from working on a story you love and the fact that you've communicated it effectively. Those kinds of stories don't come along all the time, but when one does, it makes everything else a lot more tolerable."

Troy Anderson

Troy Anderson is an investigative reporter at the *Los Angeles Daily News*, where he mainly covers Los Angeles County government.

"I graduated from the University of Oregon in 1991 with a bachelor of science degree in news-editorial journalism and a minor in political science," says Anderson. "In college, I worked as a freelance writer for the *Oregon Daily Emerald* and as a hometown writer for the University of Oregon news bureau. Before graduating, I had an internship as a reporter at the five-thousand-circulation *Cottage Grove Sentinel*. In September 1991, I started my first full-time newspaper reporting job at a fifteen-thousand-circulation daily, the *Nevada Appeal* in Carson City, Nevada. I started out as a police reporter and two and a half years later was promoted to Douglas County bureau chief.

"In 1995, I was promoted again to capital bureau chief, covering the Nevada legislature and state government. Under the tutelage of an irascible but lovable city editor, I learned the art of digging and decided I wanted to become an investigative reporter. I wrote numerous investigative stories and won numerous awards in Nevada.

"In 1996, I took a job as a crime-and-justice team reporter for the *Mail Tribune* in Medford, Oregon. A series of stories I wrote on police brutality and racism led to the resignation of the police chief and a governor-appointed task force to deal with the situation. The next year, I took a job as a city hall reporter covering Fontana for the eighty-thousand-circulation *Inland Valley Daily Bulletin*. At that newspaper, I wrote a five-part series on how pesticides were triggering fatal heart arrhythmia in children on school grounds. The series won a national first-place award.

"In 1999, I took a job at the 220,000-circulation *Los Angeles Daily News*. I was soon promoted to cover Los Angeles County government and write investigative projects. I've won numerous awards here working out of a bureau in downtown Los Angeles.

"I cover the county board of supervisors, county government, transportation, and courts, and I search out my own investigative projects. The beat is really not as demanding as it sounds, so I spend about half my time working on investigative or enterprise stories. I'm currently working on a series on the county's foster care system.

"The biggest challenge in investigative reporting is not obtaining the information but organizing the vast amounts gathered and then writing a compelling story. The secret involves spotting the small clues in interviews and documents that hint at much larger issues. It takes a certain amount of connecting the dots and seeing through the spin. Clairvoyance helps. Actually, it's the most interesting job on the planet!

"If you want to make lots of money, choose a different occupation. Although investigative reporters are paid more than most reporters, the pay is relatively modest. Reporters at the really large newspapers make $50,000 to $70,000 a year. Editors at large dailies can make upwards of $250,000 per year.

"I would advise individuals who are interested in this field to work on your school newspaper and get as many internships as possible. It will jump-start your career substantially.

"I've always been a conscientious person, and I wanted a career that would both be interesting and allow me to right some of the wrongs in the world. Writing investigative stories can be an influential tool in making the world a better place. What could be more important?"

Dan Levine

Dan Levine is a staff writer at the *Hartford Advocate* in Hartford, Connecticut, and he has also been an editorial intern at the *Village Voice* and a reporter at the *Lakeville (Connecticut) Journal*. He received a bachelor of arts degree from McGill University, where he majored in history and political science.

"A few months before graduating from McGill, I realized I would need a real job soon," says Levine. "Since I enjoy writing and have always been very interested in politics, I thought I might like newspapers. So, I walked into my university weekly and asked if they needed something done. They assigned me a story, and I loved it. I wrote a few more for that paper, and then I applied for journalism internships and got one at the *Village Voice* in New York City. I did research for staff writers and editors and managed to get a few of my own stories in the paper. On the strength of those clips, I got my first staff job at the *Lakeville Journal*, a small paper in northwest Connecticut. I was there for a little more than a year and learned the fundamentals of reporting. Then I came to the *Advocate*.

"I am responsible for weekly coverage of the Connecticut state capital and Hartford city politics. We are an alternative weekly, so I have lots of freedom in what I choose to write about, and we can be creative in our writing style. I also do investigative news and write cover-length pieces (three thousand to four thousand words) on a range of issues and contribute dining reviews, sports pieces, music, and lifestyle stories as well.

"The biggest surprise is how addictive it is to break news. I also like talking to the public. I am in a position to meet different kinds of people from all walks of life, and that teaches me a lot. In fact, though I like to write, interviewing is my favorite part of this job.

"The best advice I ever received is to never betray a source's confidence and always write in the active voice. The advice I'd give to others in this line of work is to pitch your ideas again and again until some editor bites."

For Additional Information

Investigative Reporters & Editors (IRE)
138 Neff Annex
Missouri School of Journalism
Columbia, MO 65211
www.ire.org

Society of Professional Journalists (SPJ)
3909 North Meridian Street
Indianapolis, IN 46206
www.spj.org

National Newspaper Association
1525 Wilson Boulevard, Suite 550
Arlington, VA 22209
www.nnpa.org

Newspaper Association of America
1921 Gallows Road, Suite 600
Vienna, VA 22182
www.naa.org

For information on careers in journalism, a list of colleges and universities offering degree programs, and a list of scholarships and internships, contact:

The Dow Jones Newspaper Fund, Inc.
P.O. Box 300
Princeton, NJ 08543
www.dowjones.com

CHAPTER TEN

Careers in Inventing

Inventions have long since reached their limit, and I see no hope for further development. JULIUS SEXTUS FRONTINUS

Help Wanted: Inventor

We are seeking an individual with a creative mind to join our staff of inventors. Our focus is on household appliances that can make our lives easier. We offer a full benefits package for full-time Monday through Friday hours.

Zeroing In on What an Inventor Does

Were you the kind of person who was always devising a better way to do something—or build something: a faster toy car, a better-sounding radio, a more efficient mousetrap? Maybe you were destined to become an inventor.

Inventors dedicate their lives to creating something where there was nothing. They may have some idea of what path to follow, but they really have no idea if their choices will take them where they want to go. Unlike other people, they just can't go through life making use of things in the usual way. They are compelled to take things apart, ponder upon what they see, and contemplate ways that things could work better. Inventors just can't resist the urge to explore their environments by "playing" with the things around them.

Basically there are two types of inventors—those who work for themselves and those who work for someone else.

Though it's true that the greater number and more complex inventions are made by the large research and development departments at large corporations, universities, and governmental agencies, independent inventors are still out there—creating and improving on what already exists, obtaining patents, and bringing their new concepts to the public.

However, anyone who is serious about becoming a freelance inventor should seriously consider the benefits of working for someone else—at least initially. Inventors who work for other people have many advantages over those who work for themselves. They gain valuable knowledge about procedures, systems of thinking, how modern inventing works, and they may even gain important contacts. They are usually allowed to work with larger, more expensive equipment. They don't have to do as much to get their products to the public. And they get a steady paycheck. On the other hand, they rarely get to keep the rights to the things they invent, they don't have much control over the future of their creations, and they continue to get the same steady paycheck even if they just made a billion dollars for their employers!

An independent may do some contract research and development on the side, while some inventors employed by somebody else may be working on personal projects in their own basements.

While independent inventors focus on just about any area— from the simple to the very complex—they tend to invent the smaller, more inexpensive devices and gadgets that most of us have in our homes: paper clips, potato peelers, pencil sharpeners. Those are all simple inventions, but they are important in making our lives much easier.

Qualifications and Training

Though there is no clear-cut path to becoming an inventor, here are some suggestions to lead you toward your goal. Learn everything you can about inventing, including its history and its modern applications and routines. Read some biographies about famous inventors. Try to figure out what common traits inventors have. Do you see those traits in yourself? There are many good books on inventing that take you through the process step by step, from getting your idea down on paper to making a prototype, getting a patent, finding funding, and negotiating a deal with a manufacturer.

Becoming a successful inventor requires a solid education because in order to improve things in the world, you need to know how they work now. Choose the area that interests you, major in that, and seek out internships. All inventors should know a lot about at least one area and a little about everything else. Everything doesn't have to be learned in a classroom. Read books and magazines on a wide variety of topics. Journals such as *Discover* or *Scientific American* are particularly beneficial. Attend workshops geared to inventors that are offered in your area.

Observe the world around you. How can things be improved? Where do you see that things are lacking? What items would make life easier for most of us? How can you make a contribution to society? Dream your dreams. Research areas that are relevant. Jot things down. Explore. Compare. Contrast. Imagine.

The skills that are most important to be successful as an inventor are analytical skills. The best way to improve these skills is to sign up for science classes because analysis is an important part of every class. Other good classes are history, philosophy, and English. History encourages you to identify and analyze why things happened the way they did. English is important because it teaches you how to organize your thoughts—and then how to express them in an understandable and efficient way. All of these skills become important when you must fill out applications at the patent office or when you are in need of funding and you must write proposals to solicit funds.

Other courses that are particularly beneficial include psychology, fine and applied arts, political science, marketing, business administration, and law.

As ideas come to you—or snippets of ideas or solutions to problems—start a filing system that you can easily refer to, and when the time comes, organize things so that you can proceed.

When you think you have come up with an idea, try it out! Does it seem feasible? Physically—does it work? How does it need to be adjusted? Do you know how to accomplish this? Always challenge yourself to come up with something even better. Plant the seeds of creative new ideas in your mind and see what sprouts from there. Don't forget that all inventors build on what exists already; they take up where the last inventors left off.

Inventors, particularly independent inventors, must have a fertile imagination, persistence, discipline, tenacity, an outstanding work ethic, and the ability to be productive, happy, and successful. Don't think of your inventing as a hobby; take it seriously. The work ethic is what separates successful inventors from those who merely tinker. There are no shortcuts to success.

On the Job

For a first invention, start with something simple. Then locate one of the seventy-two patent depository libraries located throughout the country to make sure that you don't duplicate someone else's idea. Each of these libraries maintains a complete listing of all patents previously granted.

Once you come up with an idea, you will need to build a pro-totype—a first example of your product. If your product is a simple household gadget, you can probably build it yourself. If it is something large and complex, you will need help to make it a reality. Banks are the usual source of financing. Alternatives to banks are venture capitalists. These people or organizations fund ventures they find interesting. They can be easier to win over than banks, but they will also want to be "cut in" as a return on their money. Banks lend you money and expect to be paid back with interest, whereas venture capitalists lend you money in exchange for a percentage of the profits.

It is smart to at least apply for a patent before showing your creation to any potential manufacturer, but you are safe discussing your ideas with a reputable attorney. If you do consult a patent attorney, the initial fee might be in the range of $500 to $1,000. The complete costs of securing a patent will begin at about $5,000 (including attorney fees). Patent attorneys will assist with the process of patenting your product and protecting it from powerful business predators who might try to take unfair advantage of you and your idea.

Independents can either license their inventions to a manufacturer or set up a company and attempt to market their own inventions. With a licensing agreement, the inventor receives a percentage royalty based upon the number of items sold by the manufacturer. To start your own company, you have to raise capital and have the management resources to produce the item. You may or may not make a profit, depending upon how successful sales are and how efficiently you operate the business.

The process can take a long time. In fact, it takes most inventions an average of two years to completely negotiate the process, and this is only if the idea is an exceptionally good one. Most go back to the drawing board many times before the process begins in earnest, meaning that it still takes a year or two to get your idea on the shelf even after you have managed to elicit some interest from inventors and manufacturers.

Salaries

Earnings for inventors can range from nothing to unlimited figures. Inventors employed in full-time research and development usually receive regular salaries (which are usually quite good), but inventors who are employed by others will never earn millions. Independent inventors have it tough when it comes to making a living. Only a small number will actually make a substantial amount of money from their inventions. However, at the other end of the scale, many of the world's billionaires (about five hundred worldwide) are inventors. They may not be inventing now, but they arrived at these levels by inventing something.

Meet and Greet

Gordon Matthews

Credited with more than forty-five patents, Gordon Matthews is best known as the inventor of voice mail. In recognition of his industry contributions, he received the Inventor of the Year award from the Texas Bar Association and an Industry Achievement award from the International Communications Association. He has also been nominated for induction into the National Inventor's Hall of Fame.

Matthews earned his B.S. in engineering physics from the University of Tulsa in Oklahoma. He began his career as an engineer in 1962, first with IBM and later with Texas Instruments, where he managed the development of the first minicomputer-based message switching system. In 1969, he founded his first company, Computer Control Systems, where he introduced a store-and-forward switching system used in the brokerage industry. A year later, he founded Action Communication Systems, where he managed the development of two products, the Telecontroller and the WATSBOX. The latter became the forerunner of today's computer-driven telephone systems.

In 1976, Matthews founded VMX to develop the first commercial voice messaging system. He sold the first system to the 3M company and played an integral part in all subsequent sales and marketing. During this time, he also oversaw the intellectual property of the enterprise, resulting in the granting of the pioneer patent for voice mail.

When Matthews recognized the need for call management systems for the burgeoning small office, home office, and consumer markets, he founded PremiseNET, formally called Matthews Communications, in 1996. The company is based in Richardson, Texas. Today, as chairman of the board, he remains closely involved in the company's research and development efforts.

"I consider my profession to really be that of an entrepreneur and inventor," says Matthews. "I realized years ago that my unique talent was to create solutions to problems that impacted many people. My entrepreneurial ability was to create companies and products that could be made profitably and create solutions and shareholder value to the owners of the company.

"My first invention was an aircraft speech recognition system that would allow pilots to control cockpit functions such as changing radio or navigational frequencies while flying formation or at night. This invention was in response to losing close friends who died while flying formation inside of clouds or at night.

"For me, there is no typical day. I try to be sensitive to everyday problems around me that are looking for solutions. If there are large numbers of people with the same problem, and the system can be implemented with existing technology, then I try to create an environment whereby the problems are solved via products or services.

"In order to do this, it is better to work in an active environment where I am exposed to many situations. Part of the responsibility of creation is to implement; therefore, significant time is spent in either taking the lead or assisting others in capital raising, team selection, product development, and product introduction.

"As far as the number of hours you spend, if you really enjoy what you are doing, you don't worry about the hours.

"The most rewarding part of my work is inventing products or services that enrich many people's lives. My work is so enjoyable to me that I can't think of a downside.

"I would advise others to make sure your real talent is to create and invent and that you have the ability to be a generalist while looking for a solution (invention). Once you have found it, you must be able to focus entirely on that opportunity until it is solved.

"How much more rewarding work could one do than develop something that truly benefits humanity in some way. Go for it!"

Daniel J. Lauer

Daniel Lauer is the president and founder of Haystack Toys in St. Louis. He graduated from the University of Missouri and has eight years of experience with the Young Entrepreneurs Organization, as chapter president and member of the forum.

Lauer envisioned creating a company that would revolutionize the toy industry and celebrate invention. He invented a doll that, when filled with warm water, was the next best thing to playing with a real live baby. When no one in the toy industry was interested at first, he formed Lauer Toys and raised the capital to manufacture Waterbabies himself. The dolls proved to be so popular that Lauer ended up licensing to a major toy company, and Waterbabies became a $125 million toy phenomenon. Lauer's success has been featured in such publications as the *Wall Street Journal, Forbes, USA Today,* and *People.* Lauer was named one of *Business Week's* Top Entrepreneurs and has earned numerous other awards and honors. He also gives motivational speeches, addressing groups on such topics as pursuing dreams, persistence, and starting a company.

"In high school, I learned the fundamentals of math and science," says Lauer. "After graduating from college, I went to work full-time at Royal Bank, eventually becoming a vice president. I learned at the bank what it took to be a 'change agent' in a very formalized structure. With these experiences as a platform, I felt I had the fundamentals to take a big risk, a big test, which is what I did with Waterbabies.

"Being an inventor is a creative platform from which to express ideas. There is nothing more creative than toys. I wanted to play a big game and influence the lives of children, and the toy industry is the place for this. Plus, I wanted to be part of a product company instead of a service company.

"My largest challenge is consistent behavior, keeping my heart and mind connected, and maintaining the high road with integrity.

"I'm not a workaholic. I like to be the one charting new waters, doing things that have never been done. I realize I have to work from imperfect or little data, but I am developing a new spoke on the wheel. I love product development—I love developing an idea into reality.

"The best advice I ever received came from one of the transformation courses I've participated in: 'Come from love, not fear.' Be. Do. Have. Life is not a dress rehearsal.

"Remember that everything you have learned along the way *does* matter. If being an inventor were easy, more people would do it. Persistence matters. And know what you know, but also know what you *don't* know. Don't get caught up in being bright; success is not about your ego, it is about being effective in the world that matters. Get out of your own way, and make your dream happen!"

Duncan H. Haynes

Duncan H. Haynes is the founder of Pharma-Logic and the inventor of a drug microencapsulation system that renders non-injectable drugs injectable. Haynes received a B.S. in chemistry from Butler University in Indianapolis and a Ph.D. in molecular biology from the University of Pennsylvania in Philadelphia. He also conducted postdoctoral study at Max Planck Institute for Biophysical Chemistry in Gottingen, Germany, and then went on to become a professor of pharmacology at Florida's University of Miami School of Medicine for almost thirty years.

After Haynes retired and the technology he invented was sold for $1.1 million, he decided to pursue his passion of telling a good story against an authentic background of biomedical science. He became a mystery writer under the pseudonym Dirk Wyle and is the author of the Ben Candidi series of books, including *Pharmacology Is Murder, Biotechnology Is Murder,* and *Medical School Is Murder,* all published by Rainbow Books.

"I have always enjoyed literature, and I had become increasingly dissatisfied with what the bookstores have to offer, particularly regarding the scientist in fiction," says Haynes. "I was surprised, though, that much of my training as a scientist (arranging compelling proofs) was so completely opposite to the demands of a novelist (revealing the truth indirectly).

"In science, the task is to solve a puzzle constructed by Mother Nature. In mystery writing, the task is to *construct* a puzzle making use of an understanding of *human* nature. My scientific and academic training has been very helpful in plot analysis; my experience as a novelist has shown me better ways to write about science.

"The best part of my job is when a fan comes up after a reading and asks me to autograph a copy of my book—and the book is dog-eared and frayed, with the spine bent from being read by a dozen friends.

"The best advice I ever received was to establish a solid basis in real life before starting to write fiction. A good novel is an entertaining but true map of reality. My advice to everyone else is to do the same!"

G. Roland Hill

G. Roland Hill is an engineer, inventor, and the founder of Contra Vision Ltd., a company in England that handles the licenses, trademarks, and patents associated with Hill's successful invention, Contra Vision. Contra Vision panels have a design visible from one side but appear uniformly transparent from the other side, or they have designs on both sides, neither of which is visible from the opposite side. More than four hundred uses for Contra Vision are in place throughout the world, including one-way advertisements on the windows of retail buildings and vehicles, building and vehicle privacy windows, and covert observation panels. Multinational companies such as 3M, Avery Dennison, and Kimberly-Clark have licensed Hill's invention.

Hill graduated with honors with a B.S. in civil engineering from the University of Newcastle upon Tyne in 1965. His professional affiliations include the Institution of Structural Engineers, the Institution of Civil Engineers, the Welding Institute, and the Architectural Association. Before founding Contra Vision Ltd., he worked on various building and highway projects, including serving as the project engineer for the library building at the University of East Anglia and helping with the construction of a major British motorway.

In 1970, Hill was awarded a British Steel Corporation fellowship to undertake research into computerized design of multistory steelwork frames. During this time he invented a steelwork joint system that was patented by the British Steel Corporation. He then worked for more than twenty years for an engineering consulting firm and supervised the construction of numerous structures, including the Olympic Spectator's Gallery and Broadcast Gallery at Wembley Stadium. In 1993, he resigned to concentrate on Contra Vision. He also founded Roland Hill Consulting Engineers, which has undertaken a variety of sports, leisure, and hotel projects.

"My largest challenge was the difficulty of commercializing a 'pure invention'—one that was not invented to solve a particular problem but that was a completely new invention with no existing market," says Hill.

"Both as a structural engineer and with Contra Vision, puzzle solving and methodical thinking are of the essence and the keys to being successful. Puzzle solving while inventing, and seeing my product on buses, shop windows, advertisements, and in the work of well-known architects, are the best parts of my job. I was once advised to enjoy my work, and I do.

"Anyone can invent and should be encouraged to try. Always assume that there is a better way of doing or making things!"

For Additional Information

Affiliated Inventors Foundation
1405 Potter Drive, #107
Colorado Springs, CO 80909
www.affiliatedinventors.com

American Society of Inventors
P.O. Box 58426
Philadelphia, PA 19102
www.americaninventor.org

Invent America!
P.O. Box 26065
Alexandria, VA 22313
www.inventamerica.org

National Inventors Hall of Fame
221 South Broadway Street
Akron, OH 44308
www.invent.org

United Inventors Association
P.O. Box 23447
Rochester, NY 14692
www.uiausa.com

CHAPTER ELEVEN

Careers in Computer Science and Mathematics

I do not fear computers. I fear lack of them.   ISAAC ASIMOV

Help Wanted: Senior Business Systems Analyst

We are currently seeking a business systems analyst for a permanent position in the Midwest. The professional will work directly with management and users to analyze, specify, and design business applications. He or she will be in charge of developing detailed functional specifications using structured design methodologies and computer-aided system engineering tools. The successful candidate will assist the organization in establishing operational procedures and redefining work flows. He or she will frequently discuss technical and business system issues with project leaders, project teams, consultants, management, and users and is expected to provide technical direction to the more junior business systems analysts.

Qualified candidates will have a minimum of a bachelor's degree in engineering, business, computer science, or a related scientific or technical discipline. Seven to ten years of experience in developing information systems is required. A master's degree in a related field will be considered the equivalent of two years of experience.

Zeroing In on What Computer Scientists and Systems Analysts Do

The rapid spread of computers and computer-based technologies over the past two decades has generated a need for skilled, highly trained workers to design and develop hardware and software systems and to incorporate these advances into new or existing systems. Although many narrow specializations have developed and no uniform job titles exist, this professional specialty group is widely referred to as computer scientists and systems analysts.

As a category, computer scientists include computer engineers, database administrators, computer support analysts, and a variety of other specialized professionals. Those in this group are responsible for designing computers and conducting research to improve their design or use and for developing and adapting principles for applying computers to new uses. Computer scientists perform many of the same duties as other computer workers throughout a normal workday, but their jobs are distinguished by the higher level of theoretical expertise and innovation they apply to complex problems and the creation or application of new technology.

Professionals in this group who are employed by academic institutions work in areas ranging from theory to hardware to language design. Some work on multidisciplinary projects, for example, developing and advancing uses for virtual reality. Their counterparts in private industry work in areas such as applying theory, developing specialized languages, or designing programming tools, knowledge-based systems, or computer games.

Computer engineers work with the hardware and software aspects of systems design and development. They may often work with a team that designs new computing devices or computer-related equipment.

Systems analysts (who are far more numerous) use their knowledge and skills to solve problems, implementing the means for computer technology to meet the individual needs of an organization. They study business, scientific, or engineering data processing problems and design new solutions using computers. This process may include planning and developing new computer systems or devising ways to apply existing systems to operations now completed manually or by some less efficient method. Systems analysts may design entirely new systems, including both hardware and software, or add a single new software application to harness more of the computer's power. They work to help an organization realize the maximum benefit from its investment in equipment, personnel, and business processes.

Analysts begin an assignment by discussing the data processing problem with managers and users to determine its exact nature. A considerable amount of time is devoted to clearly defining the goals of the system and understanding the individual steps used in the process. This way the problem can be broken down into separate programmable procedures. Analysts then use techniques such as structured analysis, data modeling, information engineering, mathematical model building, sampling, and cost accounting. It is important to specify the files and records to be accessed by the system and to design the processing steps as well as the format for the output that will meet the users' needs.

Once the design has been developed, systems analysts prepare charts and diagrams that describe it in terms that managers and users can understand. They may prepare a cost-benefit and return-on-investment analysis to help management decide whether the proposed system will be satisfactory and financially feasible.

When a system is accepted, systems analysts may determine what computer hardware and software will be needed to set up the system or implement changes to it. They coordinate tests and observe initial use of the system to ensure that it performs as planned. They prepare specifications, work diagrams, and structure charts for computer programmers to follow and then work with them to debug—eliminate errors from the system.

One obstacle associated with expanding computer use is the inability of different computers to communicate with one another. Many systems analysts are involved with connecting all the computers in an individual office, department, or establishment. This networking has many variations and may be referred to as local area networks, wide area networks, or multiuser systems. A primary goal of networking is to allow users of microcomputers, also known as personal computers or PCs, to retrieve data from a mainframe computer and use it on their machines. This connection also allows data to be entered into the mainframe from the PC.

Because up-to-date information (accounting records, sales figures, or budget projections, for example) is so important in modern organizations, systems analysts may be instructed to make the computer systems in each department compatible so that facts and figures can be shared. Similarly, electronic mail requires open pathways to send messages, documents, and data from one computer mailbox to another across different equipment and program lines. Analysts must design the gates in the hardware and software to allow free exchange of data, custom applications, and the computer power to process it all. They study the seemingly incompatible pieces and create ways to link them so users can access information from any part of the system.

Zeroing In on What a Mathematician Does

Mathematicians are a part of one of the oldest and most basic sciences. They are charged with the responsibility of creating new mathematical theories and techniques involving the latest technology and of solving economic, scientific, engineering, and business problems using mathematical knowledge and computational tools. Mathematical work falls into two broad classes: theoretical (pure) mathematics and applied mathematics. However, these classes are not sharply defined and often overlap.

Theoretical mathematicians advance mathematical science by developing new principles and new relationships between existing principles of mathematics. Although they seek to increase basic knowledge without necessarily considering its practical use, this pure and abstract knowledge has been instrumental in producing or furthering a wide variety of scientific and engineering achievements.

Applied mathematicians use theories and techniques, such as mathematical modeling and computational methods, to formulate and solve practical problems in business, government, engineering, and the physical, life, and social sciences. For example, they may analyze the mathematical aspects of computer and communications networks, the effects of new drugs on disease, the aerodynamic characteristics of aircraft, or the distribution costs or manufacturing processes of businesses. When confronted with difficult problems, applied mathematicians working in industrial research and development may develop or enhance mathematical methods. Some mathematicians, called cryptanalysts, analyze and decipher encryption systems designed to transmit national security–related information.

Mathematicians use computers extensively to analyze relationships among variables, solve complex problems, develop models, and process large amounts of data.

Qualifications and Training

Computer Scientists and Systems Analysts

There is no universally accepted way to prepare for a job as a computer professional because employers' preferences depend on the work to be done. Many people develop advanced computer skills in other occupations in which they work extensively with computers and then transfer into computer occupations. For example, an accountant may become a systems analyst specializing in accounting systems development, or an individual may move into a systems analyst job after working as a computer programmer.

Employers almost always seek college graduates for computer professional positions—for some of the more complex jobs, persons with graduate degrees are preferred. Generally, a doctorate or at least a master's degree in computer science or engineering is required for computer scientist jobs in research laboratories or academic institutions. Some computer scientists are able to gain sufficient experience for this type of position with only a bachelor's degree, but this is difficult. Computer engineers generally require a bachelor's degree in computer engineering, electrical engineering, or math.

For systems analyst or even database administrator positions, many employers seek applicants who have a bachelor's degree in computer science, information science, computer information systems, or data processing. Regardless of college major, employers generally look for people who are familiar with programming languages and have broad knowledge of and experience with computer systems and technologies. Courses in computer programming or systems design offer good preparation for a job in this field. For jobs in a business environment, employers usually want systems analysts to have a background in business management or a closely related field, while a background in the physical sciences, applied mathematics, or engineering is preferred for work in scientifically oriented organizations.

Systems analysts must be able to concentrate, think logically, have good communication skills, and like working with ideas and people. Since they must often deal with a number of tasks simultaneously, they need to be organized and detail minded. Although both computer scientists and systems analysts often work independently, they also may work in teams on large projects. Thus, they must be able to communicate effectively with computer personnel, such as programmers and managers, as well as with other staff who have no technical computer background.

Technological advances come so rapidly in the computer field that continuous study is necessary to keep skills up-to-date. Continuing education is usually offered by employers, hardware and software vendors, colleges and universities, or private training institutions. Additional training may come from professional development seminars offered by professional computing societies.

The Institute for Certification of Computing Professionals offers the designation Certified Computing Professional (CCP) to those who have at least four years of work experience as a computer professional or at least two years of experience and a college degree. Candidates must pass a core examination that tests general knowledge, plus exams in two specialty areas (or in one specialty area and two computer programming languages). The Quality Assurance Institute awards the designation Certified Quality Analyst (CQA) to those who meet education and experience requirements, pass an exam, and endorse a code of ethics. Neither designation is mandatory, but professional certification may provide a job seeker a competitive advantage.

Mathematicians

A bachelor's degree in mathematics is the minimum education needed for prospective mathematicians. In the federal government, entry-level job candidates usually need to have a four-year degree with a major in mathematics or a four-year degree with the equivalent of a mathematics major (twenty-four semester hours of mathematics courses).

In private industry, job candidates generally need a master's degree or a doctorate to obtain jobs as mathematicians. Most of the positions designated for mathematicians are in research and development labs as part of technical teams. These research scientists engage in either pure mathematical (basic) research or in applied research focusing on developing or improving specific products or processes. The majority of bachelor's and master's degree holders in private industry work not as mathematicians but in related fields, such as computer science, where they are called computer programmers, systems analysts, or sometimes systems engineers.

A bachelor's degree in mathematics is offered by most colleges and universities. Mathematics courses usually required for this degree are calculus, differential equations, and linear and abstract algebra. Additional course work might include probability theory and statistics, mathematical analysis, numerical analysis, topology, modern algebra, discrete mathematics, and mathematical logic. Many colleges and universities urge or even require students majoring in mathematics to take several courses in a field that uses or is closely related to mathematics, such as computer science, engineering, operations research, physical science, statistics, or economics. A double major in mathematics and another discipline such as computer science, economics, or one of the sciences is particularly desirable.

In graduate school, students conduct research and take advanced courses, usually specializing in a subfield of mathematics. Some areas of concentration are algebra, number theory, real or complex analysis, geometry, topology, logic, and applied mathematics.

For those in the area of applied mathematics, training in the field in which the mathematics will be used is very important. Fields that use mathematics extensively include physics, actuarial science, engineering, and operations research. Of increasing importance are computer and information science, business and industrial management, economics, statistics, chemistry, geology, life sciences, and the behavioral sciences.

Mathematicians should have substantial knowledge of computer programming because most complex mathematical computation and much mathematical modeling is done by computer. They need good reasoning ability and persistence in order to identify, analyze, and apply basic principles to technical problems. Communication skills are also important, as mathematicians must be able to interact with others, including nonmathematicians, and discuss proposed solutions to problems.

Salaries

Recent figures from the U.S. Department of Labor Statistics show $50,000 to $55,000 as an average yearly income for computer scientists and systems analysts. The average yearly income for mathematicians is about $49,000.

Meet and Greet

R. David L. Campbell

David Campbell is the chairman, founder, and senior vice president of corporate development at Punch Networks in Seattle. Punch Networks is an Internet software developer that creates and markets products and services that help people effectively manage changing digital information. The company's first product, Punch WebGroups, is a Web-based software that lets users access, share, and automatically update any file via the Internet, using just their Web browsers. Campbell received a bachelor of fine arts and a bachelor of industrial design from Rhode Island School of Design.

"I never really knew this was the field for me," says Campbell. "*It* knew. I was merely dragged along by the project once it got going. The initial concept, once it took hold, has and continues to guide or mandate me into doing things for it. But it takes a lot of time and a lot of capital to develop even a relatively simple concept into a functioning, ongoing business.

"Everything I do is a puzzle to solve, whether it's a legal contract, corporate-culture decision, new product development, or existing product modification. Much of the process I use on a daily basis to solve each of these puzzles is based upon a general design process I adopted and became comfortable with.

"My process basically has three steps. The first is initial research, which generally takes the first 20 to 40 percent of my allocated time for any specific project or puzzle. Although this initial step of my process should be endeavored in isolation of the other steps, in actuality the research phase continues throughout the entire process to ensure that nothing is overlooked and to validate proposed solutions.

"The second step is sketching and ideation, which generally takes 30 to 50 percent of the allocated time. In this phase, nothing is ruled out. Quick concept sentences, experiments, or gestures are generated and documented. Initial smaller parts or manifestations of this phase are typically combined, which themselves are typically combined again so that the result of this phase should be that at least two directions or options for a solution to the particular problem should be apparent.

"Step three is presentation or distillation, which consumes the remaining time for the project or puzzle. During the presentation phase, all of the ideas and sketches from the second phase are evaluated and filtered. In this phase, unlike the previous phase, everything noncritical is ruled out. During this phase, final language, software code and coding standards, logo colors and line weights, and so on, are established and documented. The result of this phase *must* be something that an outsider or disinterested third party (of ordinary skill in the art of the puzzle) can easily understand and use. It should also be pointed out that this is a recursive process. What I mean by that is, the results of this phase could be, and usually are, an ingredient to a larger version of the same process with a more broadly defined puzzle.

"Though there are a number of redeeming aspects of my job, the best part is the satisfaction of building things that people can use."

Geoffrey H. Kuenning

Geoffrey Kuenning received bachelor's and master's degrees in computer science from Michigan State University. After working in the field for fifteen years, he returned to college to earn his doctorate in computer science from UCLA. Following a year of postdoctoral research, he became an assistant professor at Harvey Mudd College in Claremont, California.

"In junior high school, I started discovering electronics and electrical engineering," says Kuenning. "That led me to some introductory books on computers. They were fascinating from the start. By the time I was a sophomore in high school, I had already figured out that this is what I love, and I've never looked back. My research interests are in computer operating systems, file systems, mobile computing, and computer networking.

"The biggest surprise for me is the success of the field of computer science. When I started, I'd say I was studying computers, and people would get a blank look, then change the subject. I never expected computers to be something that would one day be found in nearly every home.

"There are a number of aspects of computer programming that require methodical thinking. When you write a program, you must carefully consider all the options. For example, suppose you ask a Web visitor to enter his or her annual salary. What if he enters zero? What if she enters a negative number? What if he includes commas? What if she types her name instead? You must consider all of these possibilities, enumerate how the computer should respond to them, and plan a way of achieving that response. This requires extremely systematic and methodical thinking.

"Another place where methodical thinking is required is in debugging, one of my favorite parts of programming. When a computer program misbehaves, you have to track down the cause. This requires an approach very similar to the way a doctor diagnoses an illness. For example, does the problem happen always or only under some conditions? What are those conditions? Once they have been identified, does varying the conditions change how the bug behaves? A systematic approach to analyzing the bug can often lead directly to the cause. If not, experiments must be planned to help isolate the bug. Again, methodical thinking is required; you must consider whether you have already tested a particular condition, and you must be sure to cover all the bases so that you don't miss a possible cause.

"For the computer programming part (as opposed to teaching), I think the best part is when you have a really nasty, hard-to-find bug, and you finally nail it down after a long search. I also love it when a program finally works.

"I've gotten so much good advice through the years. For instance, I once had a boss who would tell me, 'You think your program is perfect? Give it to me; I'll break it.' He always could. Trying to write a program that he couldn't break taught me a tremendous amount about computer programming.

"My sincere advice is to do what you love. In any career path, you need to enjoy what you are doing or you will burn out. Don't be seduced by money, fame, or what somebody else wants you to do. Stick to what will make you happy. For computer science, in particular, I guess I would advise pursuing breadth. Many people focus on one narrow subfield too early or leave school before completing a degree because they can get a good job. If you study the entire field, you will discover that there are all sorts of things that you can bring to bear from outside your specialty, and you will be the better for it."

Janey Nodeen

Janey Nodeen is the president of Burke Consortium, an information technology solutions company that specializes in technology strategy and Internet solutions for government and industry. After receiving a bachelor's degree in information science from Christopher Newport University, she also participated in the advanced management program at the National Defense University Information Resource Management College, the senior executive fellows program at the John F. Kennedy School of Government at Harvard University, and the program manager's course at the Defense Systems Management College.

"I enjoyed computer science in college, so I decided to major in information science," says Nodeen. "I especially enjoy the logical, methodical aspect of computer science.

"To me, the biggest surprise is the rapid pace of technological change. Truly, it requires lifelong learning to stay current with state-of-the-art innovations. My largest challenge is managing the complexity of information technology solution development, which requires balancing cost, schedule, and quality. I have learned that one may constrain any two, but not all three, and still be successful.

"Computer science requires methodical thinking and superb logic as well as problem solving. Most clients have a business problem that must be solved, and deep thought is necessary to examine all aspects of a problem. One must identify the root causes of certain issues, not just solve the symptoms. Answers are usually not straightforward, and approaches to issues are usually multifaceted. Computer science is very logical and literal. Good solutions are often complex, and methodical thinking is absolutely mandatory in order to produce a result that works as expected.

"The best part of the job is providing solutions to clients' problems and watching employees grow and learn. My advice is to leap, and the net will appear, so I'd advise that you not hold back. Your only limits are creativity and imagination. Computer science is a wonderful field. You must have discipline, be able to think expansively, and be committed to lifelong learning. It's a difficult profession but well worth the effort."

Jonathan Cohen

Jonathan Cohen is a research programmer at the Institute for Creative Technologies at the University of Southern California in Marina del Rey. He received a bachelor's degree in math and computer science from Brown University.

"I worked in the graphics lab as an undergraduate for four years on a number of projects, which helped me land a research position right after I received my undergraduate degree," Cohen says. "We have a research team of six members, and our mission is to figure out how to make computer-generated images look real.

"My current projects include realistically acquiring 3-D digital photographs of people for integration with computer-generated scenery or special effects, designing a system to scan large sculptures, and developing techniques for real-time realistic visualization of computer-generated scenes.

"All the way back in junior high school, I used to get *Amiga-World*, a magazine about the Amiga computer, a system that had graphics capabilities that were advanced for its time. The magazine was full of articles about ray tracing and rendering, and I used to download shareware computer graphics programs and play around with them. After high school, I went to Brown, which has a fantastic computer science department with a real emphasis on graphics. I took the introductory graphics course as a freshman and began volunteering in the graphics lab soon thereafter. I loved (and still do) the thought that on a computer you can create a world that no one has ever seen before and then show it to other people and let them explore it for themselves. As a researcher, this is precisely my job: to have an idea that no one has had before and then to demonstrate it.

"In research, there are no guarantees that you will continue to be productive. The whole point is that you are supposed to have new ideas, and, therefore, you don't know what they are until you've had them. It is hard to maintain a focus and direction given that everything that you do is new. It also places a certain amount of continuing pressure on you to feel that you can never rest on past successes. You always need to be thinking of new and different things to try.

"Puzzle solving and methodical thinking come into play all the time. The guiding principle is scientific method: have an idea, devise experiments, test your ideas, iterate. Even in a nonphysical science such as computer graphics, we run systematic experiments all the time. We always attempt to validate our theoretical insights with practical demonstrations, then use these results to refine our theory, and so on.

"The best part of the job is having new and different ideas, showing people what is possible, and being on the forefront of technology. Also, for me, research is a real team effort. Almost no one has an idea by himself or herself. It's a lot of fun to try to tackle a tough problem with a bunch of bright people.

"A graduate student at Brown once pointed out to me that research does not have to be a technical process; rather, it can be a creative one. I regard my career as a creative endeavor. Roughly speaking, for a painter, the creative part is what to paint, while the technical part is how to do it. In research, the breakdown is similar: technical ability enables you to achieve your creative goals, but the technological aspects are really in service of the creative aspects.

"I would advise individuals who are considering this field to get a strong background in math. I have found that I use my mathematics education more than my computer science education. I think many people in the field would agree with this. Also, in college, try to get involved in your professors' research. Many professors are happy to hire undergraduates to work for the summer or to work on senior theses, and so on. Forgo those lucrative internships at Internet ventures at least one summer and do some research. It will be well worth it in the long run."

Jason Monberg

Jason Monberg is the president of Carbon Five in San Francisco, California. "I love technology, and I love building things," says Monberg. "When I was about seven years old, I bought a model. I had graduated from snap-together models that were obvious in their construction to detailed plastic models requiring prepainting of pieces and different types of glue. As soon as I got home with the first kit of this new breed, I opened the box and pulled every single piece off the plastic frame it came on. Not certain how to put the pieces together, I reached for the directions. The directions referred to numbers on the plastic frame that were next to the spot that each piece had been attached to. I had effectively lost the directions. 'Aha,' I thought, 'I see: rule number one is to read the directions first and understand *their* system for building.' Similar 'aha' experiences followed when it came to gluing and painting.

"Although I made tremendous mistakes, I loved the process of building and discovering, and this applied to almost every endeavor. I wanted to try before I fully understood. The understanding always came, sometimes fast, sometimes slow. For me, the process of discovering was incredibly rewarding. It's like building a Lego set based on the picture on the box, rather than looking at the directions.

"I grew up in Palo Alto, California, surrounded by technology—Atari, Apple IIs, Macintosh, and Amiga. I spent a lot of time playing games, programming in Basic, and having my dad show me all of the high-tech gizmos his company was working with. Embedded in all of this technology was the idea of the entrepreneur who used personal expertise with the computer to build grand companies.

"I went to Palo Alto High School, a great school academically, because it incorporated computers into the curriculum. I earned a bachelor of arts degree in sociology from Wesleyan University, and while I was there, I started down the economics and computer science tracks. I ultimately incorporated my computer science work into a year and a half of classes in the music department. I wrote digital fillers and algorithms to generate music. That year and a half of combining music and computers was one of the most fulfilling periods of my life, from a creation and learning standpoint. I then wrote a senior essay on the sociological impact of on-line communities as I understood them at the time.

"I have always enjoyed playing with computers, but it wasn't until I finally used them to create something unique in college that I knew I was in for the long haul. In the electronic music world, there were established ways of building systems, but there was no 'correct' music, no documentation. The only thing I could do was to try something and see how it turned out. I lucked into a technology position that required this same approach, and I've tried to stay on that path ever since. The difference today is that part of the fun is documenting what works and what doesn't and then sharing that information with clients.

"Currently, I am president of Carbon Five. We focus on enterprise technology, which incorporates technologies that have become standards, as well as emerging technologies. Our clients want something that works *and* that is better than last year's model. It's an engaging tightrope. My role is to keep one foot in the present and one in the future of two different worlds. The first world is technology. What are the important technologies existing today? How can they be applied to client problems? What technologies are coming down the pipe? What problems will they solve? What problems exist that need new and better technologies? The second world is business. How does one build a sustainable company? Grow a company? Market a company? Where do business and personal life intersect, conflict, or enhance the overall business experience?

"The biggest surprise for me has been translating this desire to remain on the line between the well understood and the utterly unclear into a viable professional life. This includes translating what an engineer may find interesting into what a marketing person might find interesting. In fact, the real surprise is that these two worlds have so much in common, but they have very different vocabularies and approaches.

"Of course, this is where the methodical thinking comes in, in some obvious and some not-so-obvious ways. The obvious way has to do with the technology, which is always shifting. We spend our time using new and standardized technology to develop solutions for clients. This inherently entails trying new things, discovering limitations, working around those, and incorporating new efforts from other developers. The field itself requires problem solving. It requires planning. It requires using your mind to find the best solution.

"The not-so-obvious comes into play with business, with translating the problem-solving skill into a tangible marketing message, a revenue stream, and an excellent work environment. I always saw this as magic, a special gift that only certain individuals had. It did not strike me as something easily broken down into problems. What I did not expect, and only recently started practicing, was that organizing thoughts around marketing messages or revenue streams is exactly the same as planning a large systems project. In fact, it is more complex, because there are more unknown variables.

"It is invaluable to collect thoughts from yourself and from others and organize them into mental models of the problem and the solution. And that's the best part of this job: bringing together several people to create a solution that is better than the individual thinking could have created. This is like watching multiple problem solvers converge in a common direction.

"The best words of advice I ever received may sound cliché, but they work every time I think about them: Your life and your career are a marathon. Marathons are completed and won by steady, level progress. Sprinting the first mile of a marathon may put you ahead of everyone else, but it only guarantees you won't complete the entire race.

"Regardless of the career path you choose, remember that the tools you learn to cope with in one field will apply to another. And there may be a more generic version of the same tool that applies everywhere. The learning that draws you in will never stop. There will always be learning, and there will always be someone who can learn it faster or who will have a better grasp. Ultimately, though, the experience gained over a long period of time can outweigh the raw ability of an individual. Pay attention to your experiences; don't let them glide softly by. And consider what you have gone through each and every day and what you have learned. Be conscious of your experience, and it will be that much more effective for you.

"The technology world is fierce and competitive. It can bruise and break egos as well as careers. In the end, though, you are only dealing with people, and people tend to respond in fairly similar ways. So take the time to understand people. This will allow you to avoid unnecessary conflicts that may get in the way of why you are involved in this business at all.

"Also, don't forget why you started down this path in the first place. It's OK for your motives to evolve, but don't lose track of why those motives have evolved."

Leticia Montanez

Leticia Montanez is a computer scientist at NASA's Jet Propulsion Laboratory in Pasadena, California, where she is a Cassini integration and test lead and also Starlight flight instrument integration and test lead. She earned a bachelor's degree in computer science and mathematics from California State University.

"I work for the Cassini and Starlight projects," says Montanez. "For the Cassini project, I am in charge of validating spacecraft sequences and new flight software. For the Starlight project, we are currently trying to develop a new spacecraft technology in order to fly spacecrafts in flying formation using laser beams to keep the spacecrafts precisely aligned.

"I started off as a chemical engineering major at the New Mexico Institute of Technology. Once I started doing some of my class work on computers, I knew that this is what I wanted to do. Also, in my current position, I get to troubleshoot human error, software, and hardware. My job lets me be creative.

"My biggest challenge was to learn how spacecrafts work and what it takes to control them. Puzzle solving is very important in my field, since I have to take things apart and put things together. And debugging a problem in software is like a big puzzle; I have to troubleshoot by being a detective in order to figure out where the problem is.

"My advice is to finish school—and never give up!"

For Additional Information

Further information about computer careers is available from:

Association for Computing Machinery
1515 Broadway
New York, NY 10036
www.acm.org

Information about the designation Certified Computing Professional is available from:

Institute for the Certification of Computing Professionals
2350 East Devon Avenue, Suite 115
Des Plaines, IL 60018
www.iccp.org

Information about the designation Certified Quality Analyst is available from:

Quality Assurance Institute
7575 Phillips Boulevard, Suite 350
Orlando, FL 32819
www.qaiusa.com

For information about the field of mathematics, including career opportunities and professional training, contact:

American Mathematical Society
Department of Professional Programs and Services
201 Charles Street
Providence, RI 02904
www.ams.org

Conference Board of the Mathematical Sciences
1529 Eighteenth Street NW
Washington, DC 20036
www.maa.org/cbms/cbms.html

Mathematical Association of America
1529 Eighteenth Street NW
Washington, DC 20036
www.maa.org

Society for Industrial and Applied Mathematics
3600 University City Science Center
Philadelphia, PA 19104
www.siam.org

CHAPTER TWELVE

Careers in Research

Every great advance in science has issued from a new audacity of imagination. JOHN DEWEY

Help Wanted: Research Scientist

Are you looking for a job—or for an opportunity? Our corporation seeks talented and driven individuals to join its research team developing the next generation of genetic analysis tools. Based in California and founded on technology licensed from a nearby university, we seek individuals who share our vision of building a world-class organization that will significantly impact humanity through biotechnology. We offer competitive compensation along with excellent benefits, including a 401(k) plan, health insurance, and health club membership in addition to the opportunity for equity participation.

We seek a research scientist who will drive the development of our core technologies through the design, execution, and analysis of experiments and assist in the development of intellectual property for the company. Publication of research findings in peer-reviewed journals will be strongly encouraged.

You must possess expert knowledge of molecular biology and cloning technology with a broad understanding of genetics, biochemistry, and instrumentation. Qualified candidates will possess excellent communication, laboratory, and computational skills. A proven research and publication record and strong analytical skills are necessary. Requires a Ph.D. in molecular biology, cell biology, genetics, or a related field. Postdoctoral and/or industry experience would be a distinct advantage but is not a requirement. For immediate consideration, send your resume by mail, fax, or E-mail.

149

Zeroing In on What Biological and Medical Scientists Do

Many biological scientists and virtually all medical scientists work in the area of research and development. Some conduct basic research to increase our knowledge of living organisms. Others, in applied research, use knowledge provided by basic research to develop new medicines, increase crop yields, and improve the environment. Biological and medical scientists who conduct research usually work in laboratories using electron microscopes, computers, thermal cyclers, and a wide variety of other equipment. Some professionals may conduct experiments on laboratory animals or greenhouse plants. A number of biological scientists perform a substantial amount of research outside of laboratories. For example, a botanist may do research in tropical rain forests to see what plants grow there, or an ecologist may study how a forest area recovers after a fire.

Advances in basic biological knowledge, especially at the genetic and molecular levels, continue to spur the field of biotechnology forward. Using this technology, biological and medical scientists manipulate the genetic material of animals or plants, attempting to make organisms more productive or disease resistant. The first application of this technology occurred in the medical and pharmaceutical areas. Many substances not previously available in large quantities are now beginning to be produced by biotechnological means—some may be useful in treating cancer and other diseases. Advances in biotechnology have opened up research opportunities in almost all areas of biology, including commercial applications in agriculture and the food and chemical industries.

Most biological scientists who come under the broad category of biologist are further classified by the types of organisms they study or by the specific activities they perform, although recent advances in the understanding of basic life processes at the molecular and cellular levels have blurred some traditional classifications. Examples include aquatic biologists, biochemists, botanists, microbiologists, physiologists, zoologists, ecologists, and medical scientists.

Qualifications and Training for Biological and Medical Scientists

For biological scientists, a doctorate generally is required for college teaching, independent research, and for advancement to administrative positions. A master's degree is sufficient for some jobs in applied research. Some graduates with a bachelor's degree start as biological scientists in testing and inspection or secure jobs related to etiological science such as technical sales or service representatives. In some cases, graduates with bachelor's degrees are able to work in a laboratory environment on their own projects, but this is unusual. Some may work as research assistants.

Many colleges and universities offer bachelor's degrees in biological science, and many offer advanced degrees. Curriculums for advanced degrees often emphasize a subfield such as microbiology or botany, but not all universities offer all curriculums. Advanced degree programs include classroom hours, fieldwork, lab research, and a thesis or dissertation. Biological scientists who have advanced degrees often take temporary post-doctoral research positions that provide specialized research experience.

Biological scientists need to be able to work equally efficiently on their own or as part of a team. In addition, they must be able to communicate clearly and concisely, both orally and in writing.

The doctorate in a biological science is the minimum education required for prospective medical scientists because the work of medical scientists is almost entirely research oriented. A Ph.D. qualifies one to do research on basic life processes or on particular medical problems or diseases and to analyze and interpret the results of experiments on patients. Medical scientists who administer drug or gene therapy to human patients or who otherwise interact medically with patients (such as drawing blood, excising tissue, or performing other invasive procedures) must have a medical degree. It is particularly helpful for medical scientists to earn both Ph.D. and M.D. degrees.

In addition to a formal education, medical scientists are usually expected to spend several years in a postdoctoral position before they are offered permanent jobs. Postdoctoral work provides valuable laboratory experience, including a background in specific processes and techniques (such as gene splicing) that are transferable to other research projects later on. In some institutions, the postdoctoral position can lead to a permanent position.

Salaries for Biological and Medical Scientists

The National Association of Colleges and Employers reports that starting salaries in private industry average $25,400 for those with bachelor's degrees in biological science, $26,900 for master's degree recipients, and about $52,400 for those earning doctoral degrees. Median annual earnings for biological and life scientists is about $36,300.

In the federal government, general biological scientists in nonsupervisory, supervisory, and managerial positions earn an average salary of $52,100; microbiologists average $58,700; ecologists, $52,700; physiologists, $65,900; and geneticists, $62,700.

Meet and Greet

Amadeo J. Pesce

Dr. Amadeo Pesce serves as the director of the toxicology laboratory and professor of experimental medicine at the University of Cincinnati Hospital. He has been associated with the University of Cincinnati for the past twenty-three years.

"I always knew I was interested in medical research," says Dr. Pesce. "So that's where I was focused early on. I earned my undergraduate degree at the Massachusetts Institute of Technology. Then I attended Brandeis University for my graduate degree in biochemistry. My postdoctoral scholarship was at the University of Illinois at Champaign-Urbana.

"To do this kind of work, you need to have Ph.D. credentials. I also have board certification from the American Board for Clinical Chemistry, which I think is very important. Certification is given to those who have the proper scientific background, five years' experience in the field, and successful completion of an examination.

"In my present position, most of the time I work as part of a team of researchers. The composition of the team may change depending on the project. Participants may include postdoctoral fellows, part-time or full-time technologists, pathologists, mathematicians, psychiatrists, substance abuse counselors, and other health and scientific professionals.

"Usually there are several projects going on at the same time. For instance, we're now helping with the clinical trials in developing methods of measurement for a couple of different projects. One project is to help pace patients by monitoring the effectiveness of the drug called AZT, which is used in the treatment of AIDS. We've developed the technology to measure the concentration of drugs inside the cell and are working very closely with the clinician and the clinical trials that are being conducted.

"Another project we're participating in is the study of developing agents that will help combat substance abuse by reducing the craving and the other aspects that make people want to continue to use drugs. In this project, we work with a group of psychiatrists and substance abuse counselors, and they provide specimens from the patients for us to monitor.

"In addition to the hours spent in the laboratory, a considerable portion of my time is spent thinking and writing. One must think things through and be able to communicate them effectively and efficiently in order for the research to have meaning. And, as I convey to my students, if it's not written down, it was never done.

"As an administrator, I have other responsibilities. I supervise a postdoctoral fellow and handle personnel issues and administrative problems. And at this point in my life, I accomplish this and keep fairly regular working hours. But when I was younger (and for many years), I worked from seven in the morning until ten at night, five days a week. The other two days, I *only* worked eight to ten hours a day. This was not required, but just my own enthusiasm showing, based upon my decision to be one of the four most recognized authorities in the field. So I set on a path of learning all I could and then proceeded to put out a series of books (eighteen) about the field. This required an immense amount of work. I tell everyone that I did this to become rich and famous. (My children always told me to skip the fame!) But as it turns out, all I got was the fame. However, even though I didn't make the money I had hoped for, it has still been very rewarding. Fans as far away as Australia have asked me to sign their copies of my books.

"This career has many other rewards: uppermost is the accomplishment of developing a theory and finding supporting data. (After all, projects are funded grants for which you must show results by a certain date in order to be funded for the next project.) On the down side, the worst part of the job is when you write a paper and it gets rejected by your peers (and you think they're wrong, and in fact you know they're wrong). However, the real issue for me is that we've done some pioneering work for people that has been fruitful and rewarding.

"Here's an example. A while back we developed a way of looking at cancer in mice, and a colleague working on cancer research sent me a letter commending me on the work. The fact that somebody would think enough of our work to take what we've done and build on it is very rewarding.

"Another accomplishment relates to transplant patients. Some of the drugs used to treat these patients are very expensive, and we were able to devise a way of cutting the cost of those drugs from about $6,000 a year to about $1,200. This means that Third World countries can actually afford the drug for their transplant patients. That's quite an accomplishment.

"To be successful in this career, it helps to have an understanding partner, as I did. And since it is so important to be able to interact with people, exchange ideas, and get them to help with particular areas of your project, you must be able to get along with all kinds of people. You have to be aware of what issues others have and be able to accommodate them so they'll accommodate you in return. I have found that this is the proper approach to a successful collaboration. It's not unlike working with others on a book or any other project in which a number of people need to extend themselves in order to fulfill a common goal."

Zeroing In on Physical Sciences Research Careers

Chemists

Chemists search for and put to practical use new knowledge about chemicals. Although chemicals are often thought of as artificial or toxic substances, all physical things, whether naturally occurring or of human design, are composed of chemicals. Chemists have developed a tremendous variety of new and improved synthetic fibers, paints, adhesives, drugs, cosmetics, electronic components, lubricants, and thousands of other products. They also develop processes that save energy and reduce pollution, such as methods to improve oil refining and petrochemical processing. Research on the chemistry of living things spurs advances in medicine, agriculture, food processing, and other areas.

In basic research, chemists investigate the properties, composition, and structure of matter and the laws that govern the combination of elements and reactions of substances. In applied research and development, they create new products and processes or improve existing ones, often using knowledge gained from basic research. For example, synthetic rubber and plastics resulted from research on small molecules uniting to form large ones (polymerization).

Chemists often specialize in a subfield. Analytical chemists determine the structure, composition, and nature of substances and develop analytical techniques. They also identify the presence and concentration of chemical pollutants in air, water, and soil. Organic chemists study the chemistry of the vast number of carbon compounds. Many commercial products, such as drugs, plastics, and fertilizers, have been developed by organic chemists. Inorganic chemists study compounds consisting mainly of elements other than carbon, such as those in electronic components. Physical chemists study the physical characteristics of atoms and molecules and investigate how chemical reactions work. Their research may result in new and better energy sources.

Physicists and Astronomers

Physicists explore and identify basic principles governing the structure and behavior of matter, the generation and transfer of energy, and the interaction of matter and energy. Some physicists use these principles in theoretical areas, such as the nature of time and the origin of the universe; others apply their physics knowledge to practical areas such as the development of advanced materials, electronic and optical devices, and medical equipment.

Physicists design and perform experiments with lasers, cyclotrons, telescopes, mass spectrometers, and other equipment. Based on observations and analysis, they attempt to discover the laws that describe the forces of nature, such as gravity, electromagnetism, and nuclear interactions. They also find ways to apply physical laws and theories to problems in nuclear energy, electronics, optics, materials, communications, aerospace technology, navigation equipment, and medical instrumentation.

Most physicists work in research and development. Some do basic research to increase scientific knowledge. Physicists who conduct applied research build upon the discoveries made through basic research and work to develop new devices, products, and processes. For instance, basic research in solid-state physics led to the development of transistors and then to the integrated circuits used in computers.

Physicists also design research equipment. This equipment often has additional unanticipated uses. For example, lasers are used in surgery; microwave devices are used for ovens; and measuring instruments can analyze blood or the chemical content of foods. A small number work in inspection, testing, quality control, and other production-related jobs in industry.

Much physics research is done in small or medium-size laboratories. However, experiments in plasma, nuclear, and high energy, and some other areas of physics require extremely large, expensive equipment such as particle accelerators. Physicists in these subfields often work in large teams. Although physics research may require extensive experimentation in laboratories, research physicists still spend time in offices planning, recording, analyzing, and reporting on research.

Physicists generally specialize in one of many subfields: elementary particle physics, nuclear physics, atomic and molecular physics, physics of condensed matter (solid-state physics), optics, acoustics, plasma physics, or the physics of fluids. Some specialize in a subdivision of one of these subfields; for example, within condensed matter physics, specialties include superconductivity, crystallography, and semiconductors. However, all physics involves the same fundamental principles, so specialties may overlap, and physicists may switch from one subfield to another. Also, growing numbers of physicists work in combined fields such as biophysics, chemical physics, and geophysics.

Astronomy is sometimes considered a subfield of physics. Astronomers use the principles of physics and mathematics to learn about the fundamental nature of the universe, including the sun, moon, planets, stars, and galaxies. They also apply their knowledge to problems in navigation and space flight.

Almost all astronomers do research. They analyze large quantities of data gathered by observatories and satellites and write scientific papers or reports on their findings. Most astronomers spend only a few weeks each year making observations with optical telescopes, radio telescopes, and other instruments. Contrary to the popular image, astronomers almost never make observations by looking directly through a telescope because enhanced photographic and electronic detecting equipment can see more than the human eye.

Geologists and Geophysicists

Geologists and geophysicists, also known as geological scientists or geoscientists, study the physical aspects and history of Earth. They identify and examine rocks, study information collected by remote-sensing instruments in satellites, conduct geological surveys, construct maps, and use instruments to measure Earth's gravity and magnetic field. They also analyze information collected through seismic studies, which involves bouncing energy waves off buried rock layers. Many geologists and geophysicists search for oil, natural gas, minerals, and groundwater.

Other geological scientists play an important role in preserving and cleaning up the environment. Their activities include designing and monitoring waste disposal sites, preserving water supplies, and reclaiming contaminated land and water to comply with federal environmental regulations. They also help locate safe sites for hazardous-waste facilities and landfills.

Geologists and geophysicists examine chemical and physical properties of specimens in laboratories. They study fossil remains of animal and plant life or experiment with the flow of water and oil through rocks. Some geoscientists use two- or three-dimensional computer modeling to portray water layers and the flow of water or other fluids through rock cracks and porous materials. They use a variety of sophisticated laboratory instruments, including x-ray diffractometers (which determine the crystal structure of minerals) and petrographic microscopes (for the study of rock and sediment samples). Geoscientists also use seismographs, instruments that measure energy waves resulting from movements in Earth's crust, to determine the locations and intensities of earthquakes.

Geoscientists working in the oil and gas industry sometimes process and interpret the maps produced by remote-sensing satellites to help identify potential new oil or gas deposits. Seismic technology is also an important exploration tool. Seismic waves are used to develop three-dimensional computer models of underground or underwater rock formations.

Geologists and geophysicists also apply geological knowledge to engineering problems in constructing large buildings, dams, tunnels, and highways. Some administer and manage research and exploration programs.

Geology and geophysics are closely related fields, but there are major differences. Geologists study the composition, structure, and history of Earth's crust. They try to find out how rocks were formed and what has happened to them since their formation.

Geophysicists use the principles of physics and mathematics to study not only Earth's surface but its internal composition, ground and surface waters, atmosphere, and oceans, as well as its magnetic, electrical, and gravitational forces. Both, however, commonly apply their skills to the search for natural resources and to solve environmental problems.

There are numerous subdisciplines or specialties that fall under the two major disciplines of geology and geophysics, further differentiating the kind of work geoscientists do. For example, *petroleum geologists* explore for oil and gas deposits by studying and mapping the subsurface of oceans or land. They use sophisticated geophysical instrumentation, well log data, and computers to collect information. *Mineralogists* analyze and classify minerals and precious stones according to composition and structure. *Paleontologists* study fossils found in geological formations to trace the evolution of plant and animal life and the geologic history of Earth. *Stratigraphers* help to locate minerals by studying the distribution and arrangement of sedimentary rock layers and by examining the fossil and mineral content of such layers. Those who study marine geology are usually called *oceanographers* or *marine geologists*. They study and map the ocean floor and collect information using remote-sensing devices aboard surface ships or underwater research craft.

Geophysicists may specialize in areas such as geodesy, seismology, or marine geophysics, also known as physical oceanography. *Geodesists* study the size and shape of Earth, its gravitational field, tides, polar motion, and rotation. *Seismologists* interpret data from seismographs and other geophysical instruments to detect earthquakes and locate earthquake-related faults. *Physical oceanographers* study the physical aspects of oceans, such as currents and the interaction of sea surface and atmosphere.

Hydrology is a discipline closely related to geology and geophysics. *Hydrologists* study the distribution, circulation, and physical properties of underground and surface waters. They study the form and intensity of precipitation, its rate of infiltration into the soil, movement through the earth, and its return to the ocean and atmosphere. The work they do is particularly important in environmental preservation and remediation.

Meteorologists

Meteorology is the study of Earth's atmosphere, the air that covers the planet. Meteorologists study the atmosphere's physical characteristics, motions, and processes and the way the atmosphere affects the rest of our environment. The best-known application of this knowledge is in forecasting the weather. However, weather information and meteorological research also are applied in air-pollution control, agriculture, air and sea transportation, defense, and the study of trends in Earth's climate, such as global warming or ozone depletion.

Meteorologists who forecast the weather, known professionally as *operational meteorologists*, are the largest group of specialists. They study information on air pressure, temperature, humidity, and wind velocity, and they apply physical and mathematical relationships to make short- and long-range weather forecasts. Their data come from weather satellites, weather radar, remote sensors, and observers in many parts of the world. Meteorologists use sophisticated computer models of the world's atmosphere to make long-term, short-term, and local-area forecasts. These forecasts inform not only the general public, but also those who need accurate weather information for both economic and safety reasons, as in the shipping, aviation, agriculture, fishing, and utilities industries.

The use of weather balloons to measure wind, temperature, and humidity in the upper atmosphere is supplemented by far more sophisticated weather equipment that transmits data as frequently as every few minutes. Doppler radar, for example, can detect rotational patterns in violent storm systems, allowing forecasters to better predict thunderstorms, tornadoes, and flash floods, as well as their direction and intensity.

Physical meteorologists study the atmosphere's chemical and physical properties; the transmission of light, sound, and radio waves; and the transfer of energy in the atmosphere. They also study factors affecting formation of clouds, rain, snow, and other weather phenomena, such as severe storms. *Climatologists* collect, analyze, and interpret past records of wind, rainfall, sunshine, and temperature in specific areas or regions. Their studies are used to design buildings and plan heating and cooling systems, to aid in effective land use, and to improve agricultural production. Other research meteorologists examine the most effective ways to control or diminish air pollution or improve weather forecasting using mathematical models.

Qualifications and Training for Physical Science Researchers

Chemists

A bachelor's degree in chemistry or a related discipline is usually the minimum education necessary to work as a chemist. However, many, if not most, research jobs require a doctoral degree. Many colleges and universities offer a bachelor's degree program in chemistry, more than six hundred of which are approved by the American Chemical Society. Several hundred colleges and universities also offer advanced degree programs in chemistry.

Students planning careers as chemists should enjoy studying science and mathematics and should like working with their hands building scientific apparatus and performing experiments. Perseverance, curiosity, and the ability to concentrate on detail and to work independently are essential. In addition to required courses in analytical, inorganic, organic, and physical chemistry, undergraduate chemistry majors usually study biological sciences, mathematics, and physics. Computer courses are invaluable, as employers increasingly prefer job applicants to be not only computer literate, but able to apply computer skills to modeling and simulation tasks. Laboratory instruments are also computerized, and the ability to operate and understand equipment is essential.

Because research and development chemists are increasingly expected to work on interdisciplinary teams, some understanding of other disciplines, including business and marketing or economics, is desirable, along with leadership ability and good oral and written communication skills.

Experience, either in academic laboratories or through internships or co-op programs in industry, also is useful. Some employers of research chemists, particularly in the pharmaceutical industry, prefer to hire individuals with several years of postdoctoral experience.

Although graduate students typically specialize in a subfield of chemistry, such as analytical chemistry or polymer chemistry, students usually need not specialize at the undergraduate level. In fact, undergraduates who are broadly trained have more flexibility when job hunting or changing jobs than if they narrowly define their interests. Most employers provide new bachelor's degree chemists with additional training or education.

In government or industry, beginning chemists with a bachelor's degree work in technical sales, services, or quality control, or they assist senior chemists in research and development laboratories. Some may work in research positions, analyzing and testing products, but these may be technicians' positions, with limited upward mobility. Many employers prefer chemists with doctorates to work in basic and applied research. A doctorate is also generally preferred for advancement to many administrative positions. Chemists who work in professional research positions often eventually move into management.

Many people with bachelor's degrees in chemistry enter other occupations in which a chemistry background is helpful, such as technical writing or chemical marketing. Some enter medical, dental, veterinary, or other health profession schools.

Physicists and Astronomers

A doctoral degree is the usual educational requirement for physicists and astronomers because most jobs are in research and development. Many physics and astronomy Ph.D. holders ultimately take jobs teaching at the college or university level. Additional experience and training in a postdoctoral research assignment, although not required, is helpful in preparing physicists and astronomers for permanent research positions.

Those having bachelor's or master's degrees in physics are rarely qualified to fill positions as physicists. They are, however, usually qualified to work in an engineering-related area or other scientific fields, to work as technicians, or to assist in setting up laboratories. Some may qualify for applied research jobs in private industry or nonresearch positions in the federal government, and a master's degree often suffices for teaching jobs in two-year colleges. Astronomy bachelor's degree holders often enter a field unrelated to astronomy, but they are also qualified to work in planetariums running science shows or to assist astronomers doing research.

Hundreds of colleges and universities offer bachelor's degrees in physics. The undergraduate program provides a broad background in the natural sciences and mathematics. Typical physics courses include mechanics, electromagnetism, optics, thermodynamics, atomic physics, and quantum mechanics.

About 180 colleges and universities have physics departments that offer doctoral degrees in physics. Graduate students usually concentrate in a subfield of physics, such as elementary particles or condensed matter. Many begin studying for the doctorate immediately after earning a bachelor's degree.

About forty universities offer a doctorate in astronomy, either through an astronomy department, a physics department, or a combined physics/astronomy department. Applicants to astronomy doctoral programs face keen competition for available slots. Those planning a career in astronomy should have a very strong physics background. In fact, an undergraduate degree in physics is excellent preparation, followed by a doctorate in astronomy.

Mathematical ability, computer skills, an inquisitive mind, imagination, and the ability to work independently are important traits for anyone planning a career in physics or astronomy. Prospective physicists who hope to work in industrial laboratories applying physics knowledge to practical problems should broaden their educational experience to include courses outside of physics, such as economics, computer technology, and current affairs. Good oral and written communication skills are also important because many physicists work as part of a team or have contact with persons with nonphysics backgrounds, such as clients or customers.

The beginning job for most physics and astronomy doctoral graduates is conducting research in a postdoctoral position, where they may work with experienced physicists as they continue to learn about their specialties and develop ideas and results to be used in later work. The initial work may be routine and under the close supervision of senior scientists. After some experience, they perform more complex tasks and work more independently. Physicists who develop new products or processes sometimes form their own companies or join new firms to exploit their own ideas.

Geologists and Geophysicists

A bachelor's degree in geology or geophysics is adequate for entry into some lower-level geology jobs, but better jobs with good advancement potential usually require at least a master's degree in geology or geophysics. Persons with strong backgrounds in physics, chemistry, mathematics, or computer science also may qualify for some geophysics or geology jobs. A doctorate is required for most research positions in colleges and universities and is also important for work in federal agencies and some state geological surveys that involve basic research.

Hundreds of colleges and universities offer a bachelor's degree program in geology, geophysics, oceanography, or other geoscience. Other programs offering related training for beginning geological scientists include geophysical technology, geophysical engineering, geophysical prospecting, engineering geology, petroleum geology, hydrology, and geochemistry. In addition, several hundred more universities award advanced degrees in geology or geophysics.

Geologists and geophysicists need to be able to work as part of a team. Computer modeling, data processing, and effective oral and written communication skills are important, as well as the ability to think independently and creatively. Those involved in fieldwork must have physical stamina.

Traditional geoscience courses emphasizing classical geologic methods and topics (such as mineralogy, paleontology, stratigraphy, and structural geology) are important for all geoscientists. However, those students interested in working in the environmental or regulatory fields should take courses in hydrology, hazardous waste management, environmental legislation, chemistry, mechanics, and geologic logging. Also, some employers seek applicants with field experience, so a summer internship or employment in an environmentally related area may be beneficial to prospective geoscientists.

Geologists and geophysicists often begin their careers in field exploration or as research assistants in laboratories. They are given more difficult assignments as they gain experience. Eventually they may be promoted to project leader, program manager, or another management or research position.

Meteorologists

A bachelor's degree with a major in meteorology or a closely related field with course work in meteorology is the usual minimum requirement for a beginning job as a meteorologist.

The preferred educational requirement for entry-level meteorologists in the federal government is a bachelor's degree (not necessarily in meteorology) with at least twenty semester hours of meteorology courses, including six hours in weather analysis and forecasting and six hours in dynamic meteorology. In addition to meteorology course work, differential and integral calculus and six hours of college physics are required. These requirements have recently been upgraded to include course work in computer science and additional course work appropriate for a physical science major, such as statistics, chemistry, physical oceanography, or physical climatology. Sometimes, a combination of experience and education may be substituted for a degree.

Although positions in operational meteorology are available for those with only a bachelor's degree, obtaining a graduate degree enhances advancement potential. A master's degree is usually necessary for conducting research and development, and a doctorate may be required for some research positions. Students who plan a career in research and development need not necessarily major in meteorology as an undergraduate. In fact, a bachelor's degree in mathematics, physics, or engineering is excellent preparation for graduate study in meteorology.

The federal government's National Weather Service is the largest employer of civilian meteorologists.

Because meteorology is a small field, relatively few colleges and universities offer degrees in meteorology or atmospheric science, although many departments of physics, earth science, geography, and geophysics offer atmospheric science and related courses. Prospective students should make certain that courses required by the National Weather Service and other employers are offered at the college they are considering. Computer science courses, additional meteorology courses, and a strong background in mathematics and physics are important to prospective employers. Many programs combine the study of meteorology with another field, such as agriculture, engineering, or physics. For example, hydrometeorology is the blending of hydrology (the study of Earth's water systems) and meteorology; it is the field concerned with the effect of precipitation on the hydrologic cycle and the environment.

Beginning meteorologists often do routine data collection, computation, or analysis and some basic forecasting. Entry-level meteorologists in the federal government are usually placed in intern positions for training and experience. Experienced meteorologists may advance to various supervisory or administrative jobs, or they may handle more complex forecasting jobs. Increasing numbers of meteorologists establish their own weather consulting services.

Salaries

Chemists

According to a recent survey by the American Chemical Society, the median salary of all their members with bachelor's degrees was $54,000; with master's degrees, $58,500; and with doctorates, $78,000.

Physicists and Astronomers

The American Institute of Physics recently reported a median salary of about $70,000 for its members with doctorates. Those with master's degrees earned about $55,000, and those with bachelor's degrees earned $50,000.

Geologists and Geophysicists

Surveys by the National Association of Colleges and Employers indicate that graduates with bachelor's degrees in geology and the geological sciences received an average starting offer of about $34,900 a year. However, the starting salaries can vary widely, depending on the employing industry.

Although the petroleum, mineral, and mining industries offer higher salaries, the competition in these areas is normally intense, and the job security is less than in other areas.

Meteorologists

The average salary for meteorologists in nonsupervisory, supervisory, and managerial positions employed by the federal government is about $59,000.

Meet and Greet

Ken Rubin

Ken Rubin serves as assistant professor on the staff of the University of Hawaii in the department of geology and geophysics, School of Ocean and Earth Science and Technology (SOEST).

"I earned my B.A. from the University of California at San Diego in chemistry in 1984," says Dr. Rubin. "Following this, I pursued my graduate training at UCSD's Scripps Institute of Oceanography and received my M.S. in 1985 and my Ph.D. in 1991. I came to the University of Hawaii in February of 1992 as an assistant researcher and became an assistant professor in January of 1995.

"Essentially, I was hired at the University of Hawaii right out of graduate school (although I spent about nine months doing postdoctorate work at Scripps before actually starting my job at UH). I was hired in a competitive search for a postdoctorate position known as the SOEST Young Investigator. This position is better than a simple postdoctorate in that it is actually a research faculty position (at the assistant level) that allows one to write grant proposals to federal funding agencies and to work independent of a supervisor. SOEST offers one or two of these positions a year, with applicants being chosen from a variety of disciplines (Earth sciences, oceanography, marine biology, atmospheric sciences, ocean engineering). Other universities offer these sorts of institutional postdoctorate positions with varying levels of support and duration.

"Once at the University of Hawaii, I entered into an agreement with our school's dean and other faculty to set up a state-of-the-art thermal ionization mass spectrometry facility for analyzing radioactive isotopes. This was a serious commitment for all involved, because the time frame for getting a lab of this sort funded and up and running is three to five years, longer than the two-year position I was given. However, I was given verbal agreement that, pending significant productivity on my part, my assistant researcher position could be extended beyond the original two-year period.

"At the time (1992), there were only two other facilities of this type in the country (outside of restricted-access national laboratories). Now there are probably five or so. Setting up the lab required getting federal support for the purchase of a $750,000 mass spectrometer. I funded it with 25 percent each from the National Science Foundation Earth Sciences and Ocean Sciences Divisions and 50 percent from SOEST.

"After successfully getting the instrument funded and starting to get the laboratory set up, I was offered an assistant professor position at the University of Miami's Rosenstiel School of Marine and Atmospheric Sciences (RSMAS). At the time (spring 1994), the state of Hawaii was just entering an economic downturn, and I felt it was necessary to encourage the university into making our relationship more formal by getting a solid offer from another institution. I would have been willing to move to another locale but preferred to continue here at UH. Following this, an assistant professor position was approved by SOEST and the UH, a national search was conducted, and I was chosen for the position. So, here I am.

"I started undergraduate school wanting to be an M.D., but during my freshman year, I became really turned on to chemistry with environmental applications. Simultaneously, I fell in love with the academician's career and lifestyle. I immediately changed my career aspirations to becoming a professor at a research university.

"I have nothing against private sector or government jobs, and know I could find some level of fulfillment in pursuits there. However, it was clear to me then and still is today that the level of intellectual freedom that the university system in America affords makes this sort of job highly rewarding.

"I work seven days a week, between eight and twelve hours a day. Part of this may be because I am not yet tenured, and part of it is because my particular brand of research requires lengthy and exacting analytical procedures in a clean-room environment that makes progress slow unless you put in long hours. But part of why I work so much is simply because I enjoy it and have taken on other nonresearch and nonteaching duties as extras.

"I teach one or two upper-division and/or graduate-level classroom courses per semester and presently am advising three graduate students (two doctoral, one master's). I do my lab research in one- to two-month chunks where I may spend all my nonclassroom time in the lab, in the field (both on oceangoing research vessels and on land), or in my office reducing data and interpreting results.

"Some of my fieldwork, which includes research on active volcanoes on land and on the sea floor, is dangerous, and almost all of my lab work involves toxic chemicals and radioactive substances. This work isn't for everyone, but I find it rewarding because of the day-to-day challenges. The part that makes it unique, and the difficult thing to pass on to students, is the application of high-precision measurements requiring exacting care and uncompromising standards to natural phenomena. Although the lab and fieldwork are both necessary aspects of the research we do, the two environments are very different and require different mind-sets.

"In addition to these things, I have also worked to get our school (SOEST) and its departments, students, and faculty online to the Internet. I developed and oversee numerous websites at our school, including interactive sites providing the public with answers to questions about science, and resource sites dedicated to educating laypeople and researchers about active processes at volcanoes and the latest research going on at the University of Hawaii. I use the Internet in my courses, and I love what it offers. Once a person relates to and accepts the way in which people make computers process and make information available, their mind is freed to cross the boundaries between the abstract and the physical. Computers are a wonderful and indispensable teaching tool.

"There are, of course, many trade-offs with this sort of job. To enjoy the academic and intellectual freedom, friendly atmosphere, youthful environment, and flexible hours, one must be very disciplined. This can make it difficult, as you must evaluate yourself and your progress frequently and cannot rely on infrequent or nonexistent direction from a superior. You must sense the expectations of your peers and then work to satisfy them while not sacrificing your own goals and desires. You must be self-motivated and take a very long-range perspective on success in the attainment of work-related goals.

"Additionally, today's academic scientist must deal with lack of funds at all levels. The golden age of scientific research died out in the 1980s (if not earlier). I watch my older colleagues struggling to adapt to this new environment, but since I never knew the days of seemingly unlimited research funds, I don't get as depressed as they do at the difficulty of getting research funded today.

"Jobs are very difficult to obtain, so always work hard at everything you do. Not only are top-notch resumes required to land one of these jobs, but hard work will be required to keep it. A university professor's life may appear to be genteel and rewarding and filled with healthy doses of wisdom and cups of cappuccino at the local coffeehouse, but it is actually rigorous on many levels."

For Additional Information

Biological and Medical Scientists

For information on careers in physiology, contact:

American Physiological Society
Membership Services Department
9650 Rockville Pike
Bethesda, MD 20814
www.the-aps.org

For information on careers in biotechnology, contact:

Biotechnology Industry Organization
1625 K Street NW, Suite 1100
Washington, DC 20006
www.bio.org

For information on careers in biochemistry, contact:

American Society for Biochemistry and Molecular Biology
9650 Rockville Pike
Bethesda, MD 20814
www.asbmb.org

For information on careers in botany, contact:

Botanical Society of America
Business Office
1725 Neil Avenue
Columbus, OH 43210
www.botany.org

For information on careers in microbiology, contact:

American Society for Microbiology
Office of Education and Training
Career Information
1752 N Street NW
Washington, DC 20036
www.asmusa.org

Information on federal job opportunities is available from local offices of state employment services or the U.S. Office of Personnel Management, located in major metropolitan areas.

Chemists

General information on career opportunities and earnings for chemists is available from:

American Chemical Society
Department of Career Services
1155 Sixteenth Street NW
Washington, DC 20036
www.acs.org

Physicists and Astronomers

General information on career opportunities in physics is available from:

American Institute of Physics
Career Planning and Placement
One Physics Ellipse
College Park, MD 20740
www.aip.org

American Physical Society
Education Department
One Physics Ellipse
College Park, MD 20740
www.aps.org

For a pamphlet containing information on careers in astronomy, send your request to:

American Astronomical Society
Education Office
University of Texas
Department of Astronomy
Austin, TX 78712

American Astronomical Society
2000 Florida Avenue NW, Suite 400
Washington, DC 20009
www.aas.org

Geologists and Geophysicists

Information on training and career opportunities for geologists is
available from:

American Geological Institute
4220 King Street
Alexandria, VA 22302
www.agiweb.org

Geological Society of America
P.O. Box 9140
3300 Penrose Place
Boulder, CO 80301
www.geosociety.org

American Association of Petroleum Geologists
Communications Department
P.O. Box 979
Tulsa, OK 74101
www.aapg.org

Information on training and career opportunities for geophysicists is available from:

American Geophysical Union
2000 Florida Avenue NW
Washington, DC 20009
www.agu.org

A list of curricula in colleges and universities offering programs in oceanography and related fields is available from:

Marine Technology Society
1828 L Street NW, Suite 906
Washington, DC 20036
www.mtsociety.org

Meteorology

Information on career opportunities in meteorology is available from:

American Meteorological Society
45 Beacon Street
Boston, MA 02108
www.ametsoc.org

National Oceanic and Atmospheric Administration
Human Resources Management Office
1315 East West Highway
Route Code OA/22
Silver Spring, MD 20910
www.noaa.gov/jobs.html

National Oceanic and Atmospheric Administration
Fourteenth Street and Constitution Avenue NW, Room 6013
Washington, DC 20230
www.noaa.gov

About the Author

J an Goldberg's love for the printed page began well before her second birthday. Regular visits to the book bindery where her grandfather worked produced a magic combination of sights and smells that she carries with her to this day.

Childhood was filled with composing poems and stories, reading books, and playing library. Elementary and high school included an assortment of contributions to school newspapers. While a full-time college student, Goldberg wrote extensively as part of her job responsibilities in the College of Business Administration at Roosevelt University in Chicago. After receiving a degree in elementary education, she was able to extend her love of reading and writing to her students. Even today, she continues to teach by presenting writing workshops and classes to both adults and children throughout the country.

Goldberg has written extensively in the occupations area for General Learning Corporation's *Career World Magazine*, as well as for the many career publications produced by CASS Communications. She has also contributed to a number of projects for educational publishers, including Scott Foresman, Addison-Wesley, and Camp Fire Boys and Girls.

As a feature writer, Goldberg has published work in *Parenting Magazine, Today's Chicago Woman, Opportunity Magazine, Chicago Parent, Correspondent, Opportunity Magazine, Successful Student, Complete Woman, North Shore Magazine,* and the Pioneer Press newspapers. In all, she has published more than five hundred pieces as a full-time freelance writer.

In addition to *Careers for Puzzle Solvers & Other Methodical Thinkers,* she is the author of *Careers for Homebodies & Other Independent Souls, Careers for Geniuses & Other Gifted Types,*

Careers for Scientific Types & Other Inquiring Minds, Careers for Persuasive Types & Others Who Won't Take No for an Answer, Careers for Extroverts & Other Gregarious Types, Careers for Competitive Spirits & Other Peak Performers, Careers for Patriotic Types & Others Who Want to Serve Their Country, Opportunities in Entertainment Careers, Careers for Color Connoisseurs & Other Visual Types, Careers for Class Clowns & Other Engaging Types, On the Job: Real People Working in Communications, On the Job: Real People Working in Entertainment, Great Jobs for Music Majors, Great Jobs for Computer Science Majors, Great Jobs for Theater Majors, Careers for Courageous People, Careers in Journalism, Great Jobs for Accounting Majors, On the Job: Real People Working in Science, Opportunities in Research and Development Careers, and *Opportunities in Horticulture Careers,* all published by VGM Career Books, a division of The McGraw-Hill Companies. She also completed four Capstone High/Low Books for elementary school students: *Private Investigator, Fire Fighter, Medical Record Technician,* and *Security Guard.*

As author of *Perfectionism: What's Bad About Being Too Good?,* she was named to the New York Public Library's List of Books for the Teen Age for the Year 2000.